THEMATIC UNIT

Peace

Written by Mary Ellen Sterling

Illustrated by Keith Vasconcelles

Teacher Created Materials, Inc.
P.O. Box 1040
Huntington Beach, CA 92647
©1992 Teacher Created Materials, Inc.
Made in U.S.A.

ISBN 1-55734-233-4

Table of Contents

Introduction

Peace contains a captivating whole language, thematic unit about emphasizing peace, not war. Its 80 exciting reproducible pages are filled with a wide variety of lesson ideas designed for use with intermediate children.

At its core is *The Big Book for Peace*, a compilation of literature selections about peace. For each of these selections, activities are included which set the stage for reading, encourage the enjoyment of the book, and extend the concepts gained. In addition, the theme is connected to the curriculum with activities in language arts (including daily writing suggestions), math, science, social studies, art, music, and life skills (cooking, physical education, career awareness, etc). Many of these activities encourage cooperative learning. Suggestions and patterns for bulletin boards and unit management tools are additional time savers for the busy teacher. Furthermore, directions for student-created Big Books and a culminating activity, which allow students to synthesize their knowledge in order to produce products that can be shared beyond the classroom, highlight this very complete teacher resource.

This thematic unit includes:

❑ **literature selections**—summaries of stories with related lessons (complete with reproducible pages) that cross the curriculum.

❑ **poetry**—suggested selections and lessons enabling students to write and publish their own works.

❑ **planning guides**—suggestions for sequencing lessons each day of the unit.

❑ **writing ideas**—daily suggestions as well as writing activities across the curriculum, including Big Books.

❑ **bulletin board ideas**—suggestions and plans for student-created and/or interactive bulletin boards.

❑ **homework suggestions**—extending the unit to the child's home.

❑ **curriculum connections**—in language arts, math, science, social studies, art, music, and life skills such as cooking, physical education, and career awareness.

❑ **group projects**—to foster cooperative learning.

❑ **a culminating activity**—which requires students to synthesize their learning to produce a product or engage in an activity that can be shared with others.

❑ **a bibliography**—suggesting additional literature and non-fiction books on the theme.

To keep this valuable resource intact so that it can be used year after year, you may wish to punch holes in the pages and store them in a three-ring binder.

Introduction (cont.)

Why Whole Language?

A Whole Language approach involves children in using all modes of communication: reading, writing, listening, observing, illustrating, experiencing, and doing. Communication skills are interconnected and integrated into lessons that emphasize the whole of language rather than isolating its parts. The lessons revolve around selected literature. Reading is not taught as a separate subject from writing and spelling, for example. A child reads, writes (spelling appropriately for his/her level), speaks, listens, etc. in response to a literature experience introduced by the teacher. In this way, language skills grow naturally, stimulated by involvement and interest in the topic at hand.

Why Thematic Planning?

One very useful tool for implementing an integrated whole language program is thematic planning. By choosing a theme with correlating literature selections for a unit of study, a teacher can plan activities throughout the day that lead to a cohesive, in-depth study of the topic. Students will be practicing and applying their skills in meaningful contexts. Consequently, they will tend to learn and retain more. Both teachers and students will be freed from a day that is broken into unrelated segments of isolated drill and practice.

Why Cooperative Learning?

Besides academic skills and content, students need to learn social skills. No longer can this area of development be taken for granted. Students must learn to work cooperatively in groups in order to function well in modern society. Group activities should be a regular part of school life and teachers should consciously include social objectives as well as academic objectives in their planning. For example, a group working together to write a report may need to select a leader. The teacher should make clear to the students and monitor the qualities of good leader-follower group interaction just as he/she would state and monitor the academic goals of the projects.

Why Big Books?

An excellent cooperative, whole language activity is the production of Big Books. Groups of students, or the whole class, can apply their language skills, content knowledge, and creativity to produce a Big Book that can become a part of the classroom library to be read and reread. These books make excellent culminating projects for sharing beyond the classroom with parents, librarians, other classes, etc. Big Books can be produced in many ways and this thematic unit book includes directions for at least one method you may choose.

The Big Book for Peace

Edited by Ann Durell and Marilyn Sachs

Summary

The Big Book for Peace *represents the work of over thirty notable children's authors and illustrators. It is a compilation of stories, pictures, poems, and even a song about the topic of peace. Many kinds of peace are explored: peace among neighbors, near and far; racial harmony and harmony among family members; and understanding among people despite their beliefs or differences in age. The project came about because of a librarian's dismay when some of her colleagues enthused over a new book about World War II. It didn't seem right to her that war, not peace, was being emphasized in books for children. Thanks to her efforts and the anti-war sentiment of others in the children's book community, this outstanding literature anthology was produced. Whether you use a few or all of the selections in this book, you will be opening students' minds to the power and possibilities of peace.*

The outline below is a suggested plan for using the various activities that are presented in this unit. You should adapt these ideas to fit your own classroom situation.

Sample Plan

Day I *The Need for Peace*

- Set the mood with A Peace Bulletin Board (pages 73-77).
- Introduce the Peace Unit. Discuss and define **PEACE** (see 1st activity on page 9).
- Read aloud "Peace Begins with You" by Katherine Scholes.
- Make a web of definitions of **PEACE**.
- Assign for reading "There Is An Island."
- Geography: Map It (page 16).
- Choose a vocabulary activity from page 52.

DAY II *Dreams for Peace*

- Assign for reading: "The Dream" by Stephen Kellogg; "The Silent Lobby" by Mildred Pitts Walter.
- Choose from activities on pages 11, 36.
- Math: A Peaceful Quote (page 12).
- Social Studies: Compare "Gettysburg Address" with "I Have a Dream" (page 10); study the amendments (page 38).
- Learn about Martin Luther King, Jr. (page 37).
- Vocabulary: activity from page 52.

DAY III *Consequences of War*

- Assign for Reading: "The Game" by Myra Cohn Livingston, "They That Take the Sword" by Milton Meltzer, "Letter from a Concentration Camp" by Yoshiko Uchida.
- Choose activities from pages 18, 22, 29.
- Math: War statistics (page 19) and North to Freedom (page 23).
- Language: Friendly Letters (page 30).
- Vocabulary: activity from page 52.

DAY IV *Sibling Rivalry*

- Assign for Reading: "The Two Brothers" by Lloyd Alexander, "The Bus for Deadhorse" by Natalie Babbitt.
- Choose activities from pages 13, 26.
- Art: positive/negative project (page 13).
- Math: Fair Fractions (page 27).
- Vocabulary: activity from page 52.

DAY V *Bringing Peace to the World.*

- Read "A Ruckus" by Thacher Hurd; sing "One More Time" by Nancy Willard.
- Choose activities from pages 41, 47.
- Language: Cartoons (page 48).
- Music: Fact Sheet (page 42).
- Vocabulary: activity from page 52.
- Plan a Worldwide Ruckus (pages 65-72).

Overview of Activities

SETTING THE STAGE

1. Set the mood in the classroom with a Peace bulletin board (complete directions and patterns can be found on pages 73-77). Write some famous quotes about peace on different colored pieces of construction paper and attach them to the bulletin board background. For a challenge, omit the quote's author or source; have students research the source of each quote.

2. Begin a current events bulletin board devoted to the topic of peace. Divide the board into three sections: local, country, and world. Instruct the students to look for current peace news stories in newspapers and periodicals. Have them share their stories weekly in small groups. Add clippings to the appropriate section of the bulletin board. Encourage students to review them during free time or other specified time. Have them fill out an article report for a story (see page 8 for sample forms).

3. Introduce the Peace unit with any of the suggested activities on page 9. Students can define and discuss the meaning of peace, make collages, listen to peace music, or watch a film about Mohandas Gandhi, for example. Choose those activities which will be most meaningful and appropriate for your class.

ENJOYING THE BOOK

1. Obtaining a classroom set of *The Big Book for Peace* may not be financially feasible so you may want to employ any of the following alternatives.
   a. Read a selection aloud to the class.
   b. Make *The Big Book for Peace* available to students on a rotating basis.
   c. Buy three or four copies of the text. Group the students and provide each group with one text.
   d. For classroom use, it is permissible to photocopy a page or story. Convert it into a transparency for the overhead projector.

2. *The Big Book for Peace* can be presented in a number of ways including the following:
   a. Choose and focus on one story per session for the whole class.
   b. Assign a different story to each group or pair of students. After they have completed their respective assignments, they may present their findings to the whole class.
   c. Group the students to work together on different projects for the same story. Have them share the projects in whole group.
   d. Create a list of assignments to be completed on a weekly basis (see the sample on the right). Give the students a choice of the story they will use and tell them they must complete three different stories within three weeks (or other time frame).
   e. Use two or three stories with the whole class before letting them choose another story on their own.
   f. Group the stories according to themes: war; brotherhood; civil rights, for example. Assign each group of students a different theme to study and research.

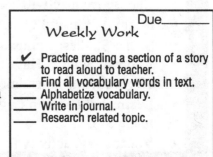

Overview of Activities *(cont.)*

ENYOYING THE BOOK *(cont.)*

3. Each story, poem, and song in *The Big Book for Peace* has been divided into manageable lesson segments in this thematic unit. These segments are explained below.

   Pre-Reading Activity. Usually this consists of a quick way to set the tone for the piece and enlists student involvement. Little teacher-preparation is needed for most of the stories.

   Vocabulary. A suggested list of vocabulary words is supplied for applicable stories. Add or delete vocabulary words as needed. Extended vocabulary ideas can be found on page 52.

   For Discussion: Some comprehension questions have been supplied for each piece. They may be used for oral or written exercises. Add or delete from the list of questions as needed.

   Activities: These ideas focus on the application of different subjects to the actual literature piece. For example, "There Is an Island" easily lends itself to map skills, while "The Silent Lobby" is a natural introduction to exploring the Bill of Rights. Choose those activities which are best suited to your curriculum needs and the needs and interests of the students. Some worksheets have been provided as reinforcement.

   Follow-Ups: These are suggested extensions for the stories. You may assign them for extra credit or use the projects to challenge those students who are capable of advanced independent work.

   Before beginning a story, be familiar with the possible activities and prepare your own plans or web of instructional lessons. Add your own ideas and delete any of the provided activities which are unsuitable for your particular situation. (See Sample Plan, page 5, for ideas on structuring lesson plans).

EXTENDING THE BOOK

1. Follow-Ups are provided for each story. Any of them would be appropriate for extended study.

2. Read more books about peace. Look in the bibliography on page 80 for selected titles.

3. Write to any of the organizations listed on page 51. Have students find out what is being done to promote peace and how they can help.

4. Find out more about the authors and illustrators of *The Big Book for Peace*. Page 50 contains a number of sources for information. Follow up with oral or written reports (see Writing a Report on page 57).

5. Read and explore some of the other books written by the authors and drawn by the illustrators of *The Big Book for Peace*. Display as many of these books as possible. Let each student choose one book and share it with the class.

6. Plan a Worldwide Ruckus for Peace as a culminating activity and invite other classes, parents, and others from the community to attend. Set up four centers to display student work and provide some light refreshments. Complete how-to's are provided on pages 65-72.

Dual Article Reports

Two sample article reports for student use appear below. Supply a different one each week or give students a choice between both forms. If preferred, make an overhead transparency of either report and have the students copy the outline on a sheet of paper.

Article Report I

Name _____ Date _____

1. I found this article _____ in _____
                        (article name)   (periodical name)
   on page(s)_____ of the_____ issue.
                                  (month and year)

2. I chose this article because _____

   _____

3. Some things I learned from this article _____

   _____

   _____

   _____

4. One thing I would like to learn more about _____

   _____

5. I would recommended this article to _____

Article Report II

Name _____ Date _____

Title of article _____

Name of periodical _____

Date of issue_____page(s)_____ to_____

Summary of article _____

_____

_____

What I learned from this article _____

_____

_____

_____

One thing I did not agree with in the article _____

Introducing the Peace Unit

There are as many ways to introduce a unit on Peace as there are definitions for peace itself. Below is a sampling of ideas and activities that you can employ to begin the unit. Choose those projects which best suit your teaching style and classroom needs.

☮ Give each student a 3"x 5"(8 cm x 13 cm) index card (or cut construction paper rectangles). Write PEACE in large block letters on the chalkboard. Direct the students to write a definition of peace. Have the students exchange cards. Read the definitions aloud and discuss them.

☮ Read aloud the book *Peace Begins with You* by Katherine Scholes, (Sierra Club Books, 1989) or type the entire text onto one or two pages, group the students, and give each group a copy of the text to read. Once the text has been read, tell students to write their impressions using descriptive words and phrases, e.g., thought-provoking, food for thought, insightful, etc. Note: If desired, word-process the text on the classroom computer; students can read the story on the monitor. Make an overhead transparency of the typed text so that all the students can see the text at once.

☮ Draw a book shape (see diagram at right) on butcher paper. Cut out and write a title across the top using bold letters. Attach to a prepared bulletin board background. Have students write on the open book page various ways to encourage peace. (See pages 73 to 77 for complete directions on constructing this bulletin board).

☮ Display a variety of peace symbols (See page 63 for some graphics). Discuss the meaning and origin of each symbol.

☮ Divide the students into groups of three or four. Supply each group with magazines, newspapers, scissors, a piece of cardboard or tagboard, and glue. Direct the groups to find and cut out pictures and words that convey peace. Glue them to the cardboard. When all the groups have a finished product, share them within the whole group. Display on a classroom wall.

☮ Record yourself, or a student volunteer, reading Martin Luther King, Jr.'s "I Have a Dream" speech. Have the class listen to the tape. Discuss any lines which may be familiar to them; what is the origin of these lines? Establish that some are based on Lincoln's "Gettysburg Address", while other lines are reminiscent of the song *My Country 'Tis of Thee*. As a prelude or a follow-up to this activity, have student pairs compare and contrast King's "I Have a Dream" speech with Lincoln's "Gettysburg Address" (see page 10). For complete transcripts of both speeches use *More Classics to Read Aloud to Your Children* compiled by William F. Russell, Ed. D., (Crown Publishers, 1986).

☮ Watch the 1982 Oscar-winning film, *Gandhi*. Check your local school system's media center for availability or a public library, university or college library, or a video store. Discuss the irony of his life (advocating peace, yet dying from a violent act), what the students may have learned from his life, and if they would be willing to live as austerely for a cause that they believed in.

☮ Listen to or learn some appropriate music about peace from hymns to rock music. Sample titles and artists include *If I Can Dream* (sung by Elvis Presley); *From a Distance* (sung by Bette Midler); the hymn *Let There Be Peace on Earth*. Other songs can be found in *Tom Glazer's Songs of Peace, Freedom, and Protest* (David McKay Company, Incorporated, 1970).

Two Great Speeches

Before beginning this exercise you will need to have copies available of Lincoln's "Gettysburg Address" and Martin Luther King, Jr.'s "I Have a Dream" speech. Both can be found in the book *More Classics to Read Aloud to Your Children* compiled by William F. Russell, Ed. D. (Crown Publishers, Incorporated, 1989). Other sources include history texts, encyclopedias, or books about Lincoln and King. Make enough copies for each pair of students or create an overhead transparency for all to view. A third alternative is to assign students to find copies of the speeches.

Once the students are prepared, distribute the quiz below. Assign pairs, small groups, or individuals to complete the worksheet. The quiz may also be administered orally. Direct the students to number a sheet of paper from one to twelve. After each number write G if the correct answer is the "Gettysburg Address"; write a D if the correct answer is the "I Have a Dream" speech.

Fill in the G circle if the "Gettysburg Address" is the correct answer; fill in the D circle if the correct answer is the "I Have a Dream" speech. In which speech...

1. (G) (D) are we *"... engaged in a great civil war?"*

2. (G) (D) does it begin with the words *"Five score years ago...?"*

3. (G) (D) is there a *"call for freedom to ring from every mountainside?"*

4. (G) (D) does the speaker dream of a nation where his children *"...will not be judged by the color of their skin?"*

5. (G) (D) is the nation *"...dedicated to the proposition that all men are created equal?"*

6. (G) (D) was the nation... *"conceived in liberty...?"*

7. (G) (D) are we *"... all of God's children...?"*

8. (G) (D) does it begin with, *"Four score and seven years ago...?"*

9. (G) (D) are we told *"Now is the time to make real the promises of democracy?"*

10. (G) (D) do these words appear: *"...government of the people, by the people, and for the people...?"*

11. (G) (D) will *"The world will little note, nor long remember, what we say here...?"*

12. (G) (D) must we *"...not allow our creative protest to degenerate into physical violence?"*

Which speech is older? Which speech is longer?

"The Dream"

by Stephen Kellogg

Pre-Reading Activity: Write the following unfinished sentence on the chalkboard or overhead projector. "If everyone has the same dream..." Call on students to finish the sentence. Compare the responses with the actual text.

For Discussion: The author, Stephen Kellogg, says "If everyone has the same dream, it might come true." What do you think he means? Do you agree or disagree with Mr. Kellogg's statement? Is it achievable? Why or why not? What signs of peace are evident in his illustrations?

Activities:

- Create a class mural which depicts a peaceable world. Display the finished product on a classroom wall or take the mural on a walking tour through other classrooms.

- Divide the students into pairs or small groups. Direct them to write one or two paragraphs describing a peaceable world.

- Make a chart of all the pros and cons of world peace. Brainstorm ideas with the class and record appropriate responses on the chalkboard or chart paper.

World Peace	
Pros	**Cons**
• No more war • People will no longer live in fear	• Loss of income from weapon manufacturing

- Tell the students to describe a dream they might envision about peace. Have them draw pictures to accompany their dreams.

- Write stories about the picture on page 5 of *The Big Book for Peace*. Students can work individually or in pairs on this project.

- Listen to John Lennon's recording "Imagine". Tell the students to write the lyrics to their own "Imagine" song. (Also in book form, *Imagine* by John Lennon, Carol Publishing Group, 1971)

Follow-Ups:

- Complete the Peaceful Quote worksheet on page 12. Then read some other quotes about peace. Use a resource book such as *The New International Dictionary of Quotations* selected by Hugh Rawson and Margaret Miner (Signet, 1986). Discuss what each quote means. Find out something about the person who made each quote.

- Read *Just a Dream* by Chris Van Allsburg (Houghton Mifflin, 1990). Compare and contrast it with Stephen Kellogg's "The Dream" in a Venn diagram.

- Other books to read by Stephen Kellogg:

    Island of the Skog (Dial Press, 1976). Cats are making life miserable in the neighborhood so a group of mice set off to sea. They discover and move to an island only to find that it is already inhabited. They fear they must prepare for war.

    Much Bigger than Martin (Dial Press, 1976). A story of sibling rivalry that results when one brother is bigger than the other.

A Peaceful Quote

Figure out this quote about peace by solving the math problems below each line. Find the letter in the box (at the bottom of the page) that corresponds with the answer number. Write the letter on the line.
Hint: This quote is from a speech given by Franklin Delano Roosevelt.

___ ___ ___ ___ ___ , ___ ___ ___ ___
29 x 10 10 x 16 21 x 10 10 x 18 10 x 20   10 x 23 26 x 10 10 x 15 24 x 10

___ ___ ___ ___ ___ ___ y ,
18 x 10 10 x 22 10 x 17 13 x 10 10 x 19 25 x 10

___ ___ ___ ___ ___ ___ ___ ___
31 x 10 10 x 24 12 x 10 10 x 26 10 x 27 14 x 10   10 x 21 10 x 25

___ ___ ___ ___ .
22 x 10 10 x 30 11 x 10 16 x 10

M	G	P	L	H
110	120	290	230	220
A	E	B	A	N
170	240	310	210	270
T	I	S	O	E
250	260	140	300	200
K	C	E	I	R
150	180	160	190	130

* Explain what is meant by this quote.

"The Two Brothers"

by Lloyd Alexander

Pre-Reading Activity: Tell the students that the story involves two brothers and a piece of property that they jointly inherit. Have the students predict possible story conflicts. Record these predictions on the chalkboard or chart paper and save for later use.

Vocabulary: Ninniaw; Pebbiaw; willed; arose; generous-hearted; stronghold; fond; cutlets; snare; dainties; lavish; delicacies; coddled; poached; modest; esteem; splendid; provisions; dwindle; larder; ramparts; rascal; prudent; volley; indignation; battlements; shrewder; folly; ruffians; surly; contrary; brandishing; dumbstruck; befuddled; trudged; dimwitted (For vocabulary-building ideas see page 52).

For Discussion: Do you think that the brothers were more concerned about one another or about having the most of everything? How would you have solved the dilemma of one castle and two brothers? Do you ever try to out-do any of your friends or siblings? Why? How do you usually settle your differences?

Activities:

- Compare predicted story conflicts with actual story conflicts. Write a new conflict using a predicted story event that did not happen.

- Create a comic strip to map the main events of the story.

- In this tale, only one question arose: Which brother should keep the castle and which one should move? Rewrite the story by changing this one question.

- Write the list of vocabulary words (from above) on the chalkboard or overhead projector so that all students can view them clearly. As you read the story aloud, have students raise their hands when they hear a vocabulary word. Call on a student to define the word.

- Complete the Two Brothers Crossword Puzzle on page 14.

- Examine the illustration on page 14 and 15 of *The Big Book for Peace*. What similarities can be noted about both pages? What are the differences?

- Have students make a Positive/Negative art project.

Materials: two contrasting colors of construction paper; scissors, glue; tape

Directions:

Cut each sheet of construction paper in half; tape two opposite colors together and reserve the remaining halves. Place the remaining halves on top of one another and cut out a design. Glue each design piece to its contrasting background.

Follow-Ups:

- Read *Castle* by David Macaulay (Houghton Mifflin, 1977).

- Find out the names of some other books that Lloyd Alexander has authored; read one or more of them.

Name _____

Two Brothers Crossword Puzzle

Replace the **bold-faced** word in each sentence with one from the Word Bank that has nearly the same meaning. Write the new word on the line provided. Then write it in the proper space in the puzzle below.

Word Bank

dumbstruck	willed	larder	snare	trudged	dimwitted
stronghold	folly	lavish	wicked	dainties	dwindle

1. Pebbiaw frowned at the almost bare shelves of his **pantry** _____.

2. The brothers **walked** _____ back to their heaps of rubble.

3. Ninniaw stopped inviting his brother to dinner when he saw his provisions **shrink** _____.

4. Pebbiaw told his brother the world was full of **evil** _____ folks.

5. Both brothers agreed to tear down the old **fortress** _____.

6. Ninniaw promised his brother **delicacies** _____ to match his affection for him.

7. The castle was **bequeathed** _____ to the brothers by their father.

8. After the battle the brothers were **speechless** _____ upon seeing the debris.

9. Ninniaw sent forecasters to hunt and **trap** _____ game from the woods.

10. Each brother wondered how the other could have been so **stupid** _____.

11. Pebbiaw spread out an even more **abundant** _____ feast for his brother.

12. Ninniaw ordered warriors to climb trees to watch his brother's **foolishness** _____.

Which three words in the Word Bank are compound?

1. _____

2. _____

3. _____

"There Is an Island"

by Jean Fritz

Pre-Reading Activity: Have the students find Siberia on a map or globe. Examine its proximity to Russia and North America. Explain that the setting of this particular story is Siberia.

Vocabulary: continent; straddling; Sivuqaq; ruffs; perched; vie; elders; petition; rituals; kinship; famine; astounding; ruffled; nonmilitary zone; representatives; traditional
(For vocabulary-building ideas see page 52).

For Discussion: In your own words, retell the Eskimo story of how the St. Lawrence Island came to be. Name some things the Yupik Eskimos shared with the Siberian Yupiks. Describe the competitive games the men participated in during June and July. Explain why the Yupiks felt a kinship with the whale, the walrus, and the seal. Discuss the impact of World War II on their daily life. What contributions did the Inuit Interpolar Conference make to restoring old relations?

Activities:

- Draw and label a map of Siberia, North America, St. Lawrence Island, and Russia. You may want to use the mapping worksheet on page 16.

- Find out about the International Date Line. Locate it on a map or globe. Explain what happens when the line is crossed.

- With a partner, choreograph a Yupik dance. Present it to the class.

- Observe the illustration on page 27 of *The Big Book for Peace*.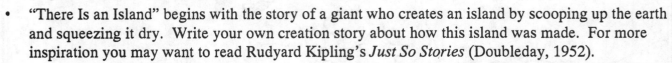
  What story is being told? Write your story on an "animal hide."
  To make the hide, open up a paper grocery or lunch bag and tear
  the edges in a ragged design. Paint the outside edges with brown
  tempera paint; allow to dry before writing on the paper.
  (A pattern for the animal hide can be found on page 17).

- "There Is an Island" begins with the story of a giant who creates an island by scooping up the earth and squeezing it dry. Write your own creation story about how this island was made. For more inspiration you may want to read Rudyard Kipling's *Just So Stories* (Doubleday, 1952).

- Have a contest to see who can lift the heaviest rock. Vary the events to see who can lift the heaviest rock overhead or one-handed. If rocks are not available, use lifting weights, dumbbells, or plastic milk containers filled with sand or water. Exercise caution when lifting weights - bend at the legs, not at the waist.

- Creative writing ideas can be found on page 17. To make a template of the pattern on that page place a sheet of typing paper over the whole design. Trace the outline with a pencil. Remove the paper from the page and retrace with a thick, black marking pen. Cut out, leaving the outline intact; glue to cardboard and cut out. Students can trace around the template onto their own paper to make an animal hide design.

Follow-Ups:

- Read *Julie of the Wolves* by Jean Craighead George (Harper and Row, 1972).
- List some other books written by Jean Fritz; how many have you read?

Name _____

Map It

Label the map below with the following: Alaska, North America, Siberia, Russia, Bering Sea, St. Lawrence Island, and the Arctic Circle. Draw and label the International Date Line.

Use an atlas, map, or globe to help you answer the following questions.

1. What direction is Greenland from St. Lawrence Island? _____

2. Canada is what direction from Alaska? _____

3. What direction are the Aleutian Islands from St. Lawrence Island? _____

4. Which two oceans are connected by the Bering Strait? _____and _____

5. Which islands are closer to St. Lawrence Island - Pribilof or Aleutian? _____

6. The Aleutian Islands are part of what continent? _____

7. What direction is St. Lawrence Island from the Arctic Circle? _____

8. Is St. Lawrence Island in the same time zone as North America or Russia? _____

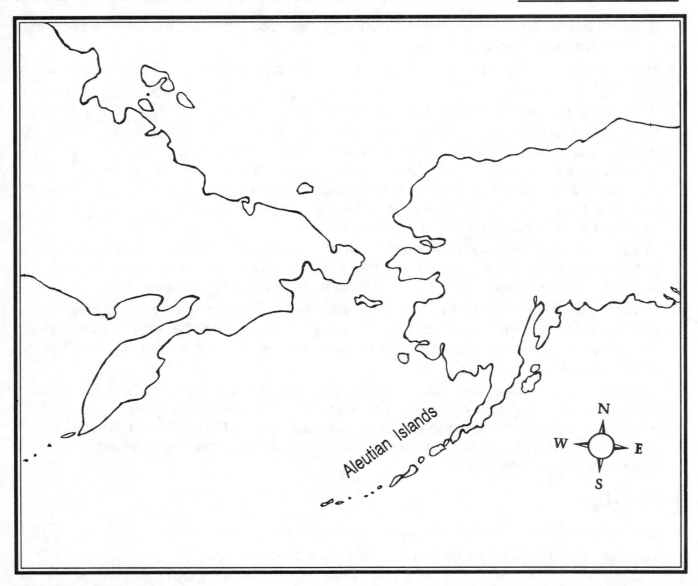

Animal Skin Pattern

This animal skin pattern can be used in any number of ways. Some suggestions are outlined below.

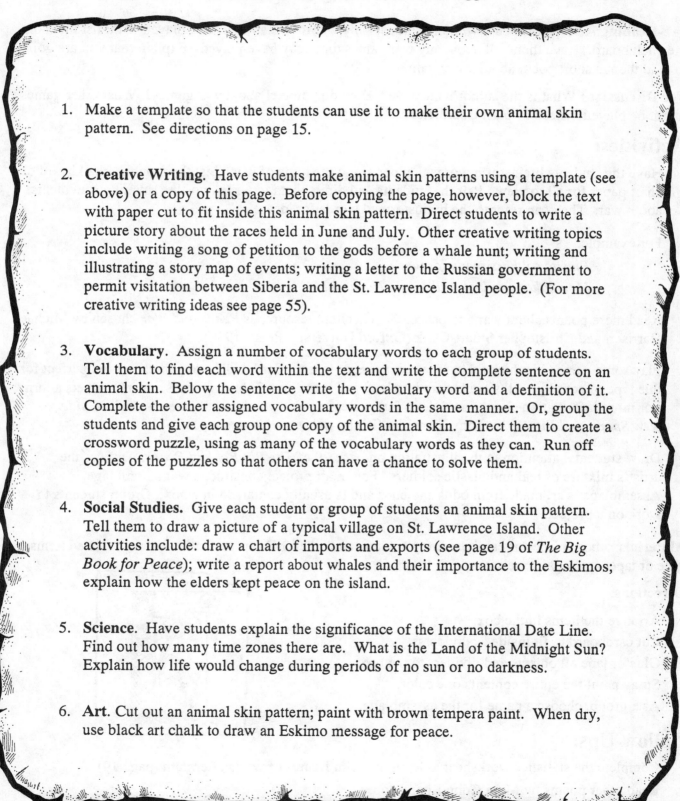

1. Make a template so that the students can use it to make their own animal skin pattern. See directions on page 15.

2. **Creative Writing.** Have students make animal skin patterns using a template (see above) or a copy of this page. Before copying the page, however, block the text with paper cut to fit inside this animal skin pattern. Direct students to write a picture story about the races held in June and July. Other creative writing topics include writing a song of petition to the gods before a whale hunt; writing and illustrating a story map of events; writing a letter to the Russian government to permit visitation between Siberia and the St. Lawrence Island people. (For more creative writing ideas see page 55).

3. **Vocabulary.** Assign a number of vocabulary words to each group of students. Tell them to find each word within the text and write the complete sentence on an animal skin. Below the sentence write the vocabulary word and a definition of it. Complete the other assigned vocabulary words in the same manner. Or, group the students and give each group one copy of the animal skin. Direct them to create a crossword puzzle, using as many of the vocabulary words as they can. Run off copies of the puzzles so that others can have a chance to solve them.

4. **Social Studies.** Give each student or group of students an animal skin pattern. Tell them to draw a picture of a typical village on St. Lawrence Island. Other activities include: draw a chart of imports and exports (see page 19 of *The Big Book for Peace*); write a report about whales and their importance to the Eskimos; explain how the elders kept peace on the island.

5. **Science.** Have students explain the significance of the International Date Line. Find out how many time zones there are. What is the Land of the Midnight Sun? Explain how life would change during periods of no sun or no darkness.

6. **Art.** Cut out an animal skin pattern; paint with brown tempera paint. When dry, use black art chalk to draw an Eskimo message for peace.

"The Game"

by Myra Cohn Livingston

Pre-Reading Activity: Discuss with the students any war toys that they have played with; list them on the chalkboard. Have them tell about any war games they may have played. Explain that you are going to read them a short poem about a war game.

For Discussion: What is the author's message? How do you feel about war games? What other games might be played instead of plastic soldiers?

Activities:

- Have the students brainstorm words that pertain to the topic of war. List them on the chalkboard or chart paper for all to view. Pair the students and direct them to write two-line rhyming statements about war. They can refer to the brainstormed words for ideas.

- For example,

    Plastic soldiers ready for war
    Mom takes one look and says, "No more!"

- Read more poems about war and peace. An excellent resource is *Peace and War* chosen by Michael Harrison and Christopher Stuart-Clark (Oxford University Press, 1989).

- Play some games in which there are no winners or losers. Earth balls and parachutes are perfect for this type of activity. All students are involved and there's no fighting because everyone gets a turn. For more information about nonviolent, fun games see *Everybody's a Winner: A Kid's Guide to New Sports and Fitness* by Tom Schneider (Little, Brown & Company, 1976).

- Draw students' attention to the illustration on page 29 of *The Big Book of Peace*. Discuss the artist's mixture of real and plastic soldiers. For an art project construct a war assemblage. Assemblage is art made from odds and ends and is usually contained in a box. Group students to work on a project.

Materials: a box; pieces of cardboard; toy soldiers and other 3-D representations of war-related items; glue or tape; spray paint; scissors

Directions:

- Arrange the items in the box.
- Cut cardboard to fit inside as dividers.
- Glue or tape all objects and dividers to the box.
- Spray paint the entire contents one color.
- As a group, choose a name for the assemblage.

Follow-Ups:

- Complete the statistics worksheet to learn the grim figures of war's aftermath (page 19).
- Read other poems by Myra Cohn Livingston.

Name _____

Grim War Statistics

Each of the sentences below contains statistics about casualties during six of the most recent U.S. wars. Read the sentences; then write each numeral in expanded notation. For example, the expanded notation of 5761 would be 5,000 + 700 + 60 + 1.

1. During the Spanish-American War in 1848, 4,108 soldiers died.

    4,108 = _____

2. World War II lasted five years during which there were 1,078,162 casualties.

    1,078,162 = _____

3. Throughout the nine years of the Vietnam conflict 211,324 died.

    211,324 = _____

4. In the four years of the Civil War approximately 363,847 Union forces were killed.

    363,847 = _____

    About 133,821 Confederate forces were killed.

    133,821 = _____

5. The three years of the Korean War netted 157,530 dead.

    157,530 = _____

6. World War I saw 320,710 casualties.

    320,710 = _____

- -

Use information contained in the questions above to solve the problems below.

A. Which war lasted the longest? _____	E. What is the total number of Union and Confederate forces killed during the Civil War? _____
B. Which war had the most casualties? _____	F. What is the average number of casualties per year during the five years of World War II? _____
C. What is the average number killed each year during the Korean War? _____	G. On the average, how many casualties were there each year of the Vietnam conflict? _____
D. What is the difference between the war with the most casualties and the war with the least casualties? _____	H. What is the difference between the number of casualties between the Korean War and World War I? _____

"The Tree House"

by Lois Lowry

Pre-Reading Activity: Discuss with students their experiences with tree houses. Have them tell who built it, how they reached it, who they allowed in it, etc. Tell the class you are going to read them a story about two girls, each of whom had a tree house.

Vocabulary: peered; prop; jiggled; weathered; shag; blunt; portraits

For Discussion: Why do you think Chrissy put a "Keep Out" sign on her tree house? Why do you think Leah told Chrissy she hated her? Why did Chrissy laugh at Leah's tree house? Do you think that was an appropriate response? Explain how the girls finally broke the silence between them. Do you agree or disagree with Chrissy's response to Leah's question—that the very best part of a tree house is the bridge. Which tree house would you prefer? Why?

Activities:

- Based on the descriptions given in the story, draw and color pictures of Chrissy's and Leah's tree houses.

- In your own words, tell about an event in the story that showed how the girls played cooperatively. Then write about an incident in which you and a friend played together cooperatively.

- Write step-by-step directions for building a tree house. Illustrate each step.

- Make a chart comparing the two tree houses (see the sample at right). Write a list of the ways in which the two tree houses were alike, or make an Alike and Different chart. Answer the following questions: Were the tree houses more alike or more different? Which one would you prefer? What's the best thing about Chrissy's tree house? Leah's?

Chrissy's	Leah's
Built by her grandpa	Built by her dad
Had a shag rug	Had curtains
Painted bright colors	Pictures on the walls

- As an alternative to the above assignment, have students complete the Venn diagram on page 21.

- Leah's family didn't have extra money to buy new boards or paint or hinges. If you didn't have money to buy new materials to build a tree house, what materials could you substitute? Be creative!

- Design a tree house that you would like to have. Draw floor plans to show the furnishings you'd like in your house.

- Chrissy wondered what it would be like to be in a tree house with no books at all. She empathized with Leah by trying to imagine what Leah was feeling. Write about a time when you have empathized with someone else's feelings.

Follow-Ups:

- Read the story *The Little Red Hen*. How would the story have been different if the characters had cooperated?

- Read another story about friendship and "building bridges" - *Bridge to Terabithia* by Katherine Paterson (Harper, 1977).

Name _____

Two Tree Houses

Compare Chrissy's tree house with Leah's tree house by writing the phrases below in the correct spaces of the circles.

- portraits of beautiful women
- KEEP OUT! sign
- two fat pillows
- curtains at the windows

- a bowl of fruit
- small rug with fringe
- built with wood boards
- walls painted bright blue

- two shiny brass hinges
- small brass bell that rang
- boards were crooked
- had a ladder to her tree house

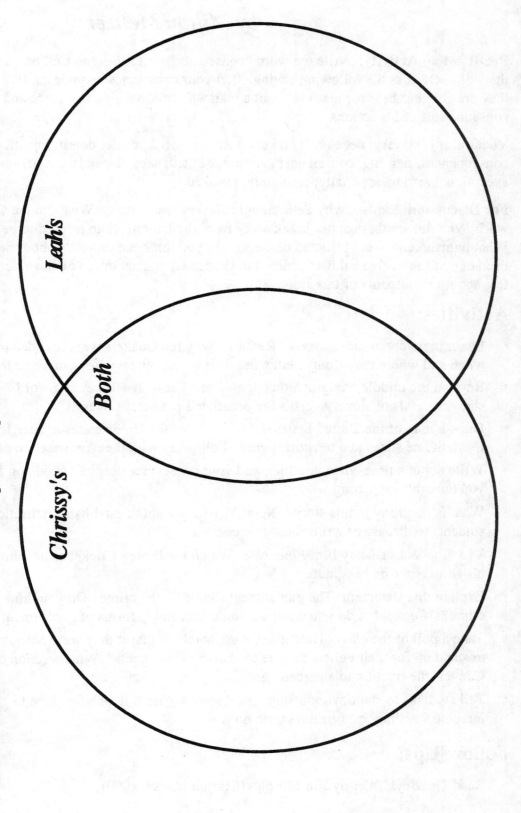

Leah's

Both

Chrissy's

"They That Take the Sword"

by Milton Meltzer

Pre-Reading Activity: Write the word "conscience" on the board. Call on various students to define the word. Discuss the following saying: "Let your conscience be your guide." Establish that the story they are about to hear (or read) is about a man who follows his conscience and faces the dire consequences of his actions.

Vocabulary: slavery; decency; Quakers; sermon; perish; cycle; detest; injustice; oppose; moral; consequences; defying; conscience; garrison; drafted; sag; suspended; court-martialed; convicted; execution; cartridges; penalty; resolutely; revoked

For Discussion: Explain why Seth thought slavery was wrong. What did the Quaker's believe about war? Why did southern states break away from the Union? Seth refused to be drafted; explain why. What punishments were inflicted on Seth? Do you think the orders to shoot Seth were fair? If you had been one of the twelve soldiers ordered to shoot Seth what would you have done? Why? Tell how you feel about the outcome of this story.

Activities:

- Learn more about the Quakers. Research why the Quakers were founded and by whom. Find out when and where they flourished; what their beliefs were; who comprised the Society of Friends.

- Re-read the middle paragraph on page 40 of "They That Take the Sword." Construct a chart to show the evils of slavery versus the preacher's praise of slavery.

- Draw a map of the United States in 1863. Color the Union states and territories blue. Color the Confederate states and territories gray. Follow up with the worksheet on page 23.

- Write about a time when you followed your conscience despite outside pressures to do something you thought was wrong.

- What is the irony in this story? Note: You may want to establish a definition of irony before asking students to discuss or write about this question.

- View the Walt Disney film *Pinocchio*. Watch for Jiminy Cricket as he admonishes the puppet to let his conscience be his guide.

- Explain this statement: The punishment should fit the crime. Do you think Seth's punishment fit his crime? If not, what do you think are some acceptable forms of punishment?

- Take a poll of the class. How many students think that if they were Seth they would have been able to stand up for their beliefs despite the harsh punishments? What fraction of the class is that? Convert the fraction to a percentage.

- Tell students to stand without support. How long does it take for them to get tired? Tell them to imagine standing for 1 $\frac{1}{2}$ days with no rest.

Follow-Ups:

- Read *The Boys' War* by Jim Murphy (Clarion Books, 1990).

Name _____

North to Freedom

Like Seth Laughlin, you oppose the draft, but you choose to flee North to avoid being drafted. There is only one safe route to follow. Find this route by working the problems below. Draw lines to connect the problems with answers divisible by three.

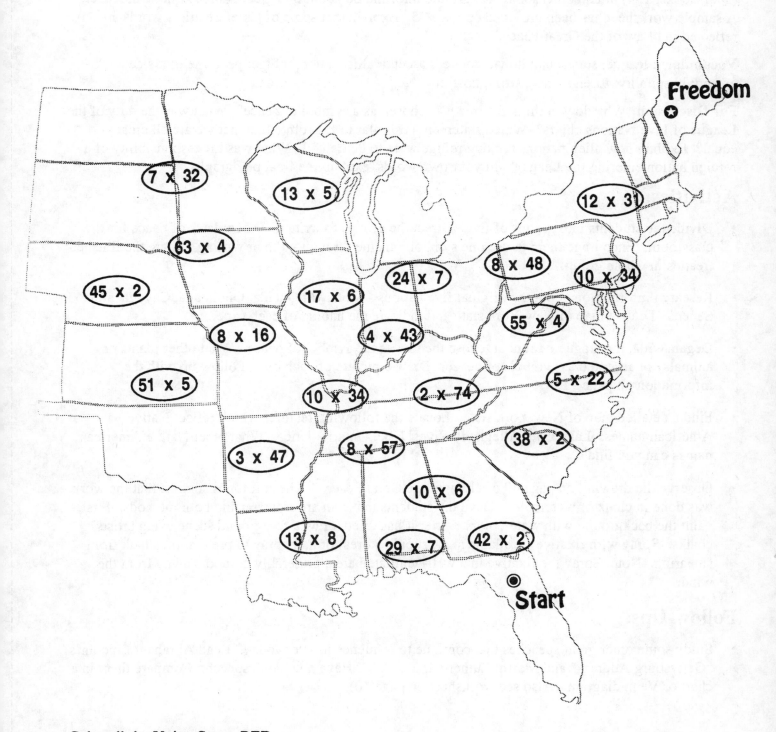

Color all the Union States RED.

Color all the Confederate States GREEN.

"Law of the Great Peace"

adapted by John Bierhorst

Pre-Reading Activity: Read aloud the book *Brother Eagle, Sister Sky, a Message from Chief Seattle* (Dial Books, 1991). Establish some background information about this great Native American leader. A sample worksheet has been provided on page 25. Explain that some of Chief Seattle's words are reflected in "Law of the Great Peace."

Vocabulary: league; statesman; down; council; ascend; allies; alien; refuge; permanent; residence; extend; hospitality; foreign; cast; strife; hostilities.

For Discussion: Why do you think the tree was chosen as a symbol of peace? What was the duty of the League of Five Nations chiefs? Which statement is similar to Lincoln's line that we are all created equal? Explain how alien nations seeking refuge were to be treated. What was the responsibility of a foreign nation entering the League? In your own words, explain the final paragraph.

Activities:

- Divide the students into groups of five. Direct the groups to write their own laws of peace for the classroom. Encourage them to use one symbolic theme throughout their writing. Share the finished treaties in whole group.

- Research information about the original five nations - Mohawk, Oneida, Onondaga, Cayuga, and Seneca. Draw a map of New York state and indicate the habitat of each tribe.

- Deganawida, the league's founder, chose the tree as the symbol of peace. What other plants or animals are accepted as symbols of peace? Draw a picture of each one. Follow up with the information on page 71.

- Find a detailed map of New York state. Locate the following features which reflect Native American names: Lake Erie; Allegheny River; Lake Ontario; Utica. What other Native American names can you find?

- Observe the drawing on page 49 of "Law of the Great Peace." The soft tones suggest that the work was done in chalk or watercolor. Have the students make an art project using both methods. First, paint the background with watercolors. After it has dried, draw a foreground scene using artists' chalks. Spray with fixative (available at art supply stores) or hair spray to prevent the chalk from smearing. Note: Spray the fixative in a well-ventilated area, preferably outdoors away from the wind.

Follow-Ups:

- Study some other great speeches that continue to influence us even today. Read Abraham Lincoln's "Gettysburg Address" and Martin Luther King, Jr.'s "I Have a Dream" speech. Compare them in a chart or Venn diagram. (Also see worksheet on page 10).

Chief Seattle

Chief Seattle was a great chief and statesman who lived from 1790 until 1866. During his lifetime, he strived to maintain peaceful relations among neighboring tribes as well as with the white men who slowly encroached on Native American territory.

As a young man, Seattle convinced five other tribes of the Puget Sound to join his tribe in battle. After their victory, Chief Seattle was honored by all the warriors. At his suggestion, all the tribes joined together as one great tribe and Seattle was declared head chief of the Duwamish, Susquamish, Samahmish, and three others. The allied tribes enjoyed many years of peace.

That peace was threatened with the arrival of the white man. Sailing ships regularly brought settlers to the area. Chief Seattle was determined to keep peace and made friends with them. He was so revered that the settlers named the town Seattle in his honor. Then in December of 1853, a governor was appointed to the newly formed Northwest Territory. He explained that the Great White Chief in Washington wished to take care of the Native Americans by moving them to reservations. Seattle's people were against these proposed changes, but, in the interest of peace, Seattle reluctantly agreed to abide by the new laws.

During treaty negotiations with the government, Chief Seattle delivered a moving speech which has since served as the basis of ecological movements the world over. "How can you buy the sky?" he began his talk. "How can you own the rain and the wind?" In the end he declared, "There is no death, only a change of worlds." Chief Seattle died peacefully on June 7, 1866.

Knowledge

Name three of Chief Seattle's lifetime achievements. Write five words that describe Chief Seattle; use all five words in a paragraph about Chief Seattle.

Comprehension

In your own words explain how Chief Seattle kept peace among the Puget Sound tribes. Explain what happened when a governor was appointed to the Northwest Territory.

Application

Why was Seattle elected chief of the six tribes? Why do Chief Seattle's words serve as the basis of ecological movements today?

Analysis

Compose a haiku poem which would reflect Chief Seattle's feelings towards nature. Propose a treaty that would be more fair to the Native Americans.

Synthesis

If you were Chief Seattle what would you say to your people to convince them that it was in their best interest to sign a peace treaty with the white people?

Evaluation

What do you think is the most important idea presented in the above paragraphs?

"The Bus for Deadhorse"

by Natalie Babbitt

Pre-Reading Activity: With the students discuss the topic of arguments that they have with their siblings. What are most of the arguments about? Who usually wins? What are some tactics they use to get their own way? Explain that the story they are about to read (or hear) is the tale of four brothers and sisters who argue about everything.

Vocabulary: greedy; quarrelsome; mantel; racket; harmony; peculiar; Deadhorse

For Discussion: If you were Mr. Moon how would you have stopped your children from quarreling so much? Do you think Mr. Moon should have given up on his children? Why do you think he turned his attention to his cat? When the children found out that their father was ill and likely to die soon, what was their reaction? What do you think the name Deadhorse represents? Do you think this was a just ending for the four brothers and sisters? Why didn't Mr. Moon worry about his children? Would you have left all your belongings to your cat as Mr. Moon did?

Activities:

• Tell the students to make a list of their favorite belongings. Have them explain who they would will them to and why.

• Divide the students into groups of three or four. Give each group some soda crackers, perforated crackers, a handful of popcorn, etc. Make sure that the amounts given to each group cannot be divided evenly among them. Direct the groups to divide the food fairly. Discuss how, or if, they were able to resolve any problems. Follow up with the fraction worksheet on page 27.

• Give the students five minutes to write about the significance of the name Deadhorse for this story, or have them rename this tale and explain the significance of the new name.

• Write a problem report. Model this idea with the class before assigning it to the students. First, read a book in which a character is confronted with a problem, e.g. *Ira Sleeps Over* by Bernard Waber (Houghton Mifflin, 1972). As a group, answer these questions: Who was the main character? What problems was the character experiencing? Who else shared his problem? How was the problem resolved? How would you have solved the problem? Write the information in chart form or use the form on page 28.

• On the chalkboard or overhead projector write the following: "There's no use flogging a dead horse." "You can lead a horse to water but you can't make him drink." "It was a one-horse town." Discuss the meaning of each saying. Have students think of other expressions about horses or other animals.

Follow-Ups:

• Read *The Phantom Tollbooth* by Norton Juster (Random House, 1966). It's filled with puns and expressions.

Name _____

Fair Fractions

In each word problem below, write a fraction on the line at the left of the equal sign. Write an equivalent fraction on the right by reducing the fraction to its lowest terms. The first one has been done for you.

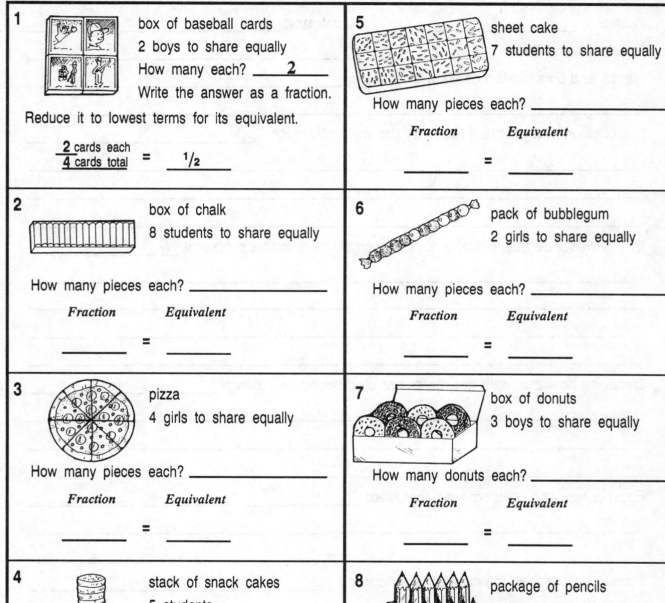

1 box of baseball cards
2 boys to share equally
How many each? ___2___
Write the answer as a fraction.
Reduce it to lowest terms for its equivalent.

$\frac{2 \text{ cards each}}{4 \text{ cards total}}$ = ___¹/₂___

2 box of chalk
8 students to share equally

How many pieces each? _____

Fraction   *Equivalent*

_____ = _____

3 pizza
4 girls to share equally

How many pieces each? _____

Fraction   *Equivalent*

_____ = _____

4 stack of snack cakes
5 students

How many cakes each? _____

Fraction   *Equivalent*

_____ = _____

5 sheet cake
7 students to share equally

How many pieces each? _____

Fraction   *Equivalent*

_____ = _____

6 pack of bubblegum
2 girls to share equally

How many pieces each? _____

Fraction   *Equivalent*

_____ = _____

7 box of donuts
3 boys to share equally

How many donuts each? _____

Fraction   *Equivalent*

_____ = _____

8 package of pencils
4 students to share equally

How many pencils each? _____

Fraction   *Equivalent*

_____ = _____

Challenge: Write 3 more equivalent fractions for each: ¹/₅, ¹/₂, ¹/₈, ¹/₁₀, ¹/₆

Name _____

Problem Report

Book Title: _____

Author: _____ Illustrator: _____

Publisher and Date: _____

Name and Description of Main Character: _____
_____

Description of a problem faced by the main character: _____
_____
_____
_____

Briefly describe the role of other story characters in this problem: _____
_____
_____
_____
_____

Describe how the main character handled his/her problem: _____
_____
_____
_____

Explain how the problem was resolved: _____
_____
_____

Describe your feelings about the outcome: _____
_____
_____

Explain another way that the problem could have been solved: _____
_____
_____
_____

"Letter From a Concentration Camp"

by Yoshiko Uchida

Pre-Reading Activity: Read aloud a section of your choice from *Dear Mr. Henshaw* by Beverly Cleary (Putnam, 1977). Establish that this book was written as a series of letters. Explain that the section they are about to read (or hear) is also written in a letter style.

Vocabulary: mailing address; cot; mess hall; soup kitchen; genuine; regret; betrayed; executive; concentration camp; Bill of Rights; due process; hearing; uprooted; ancestry; "assembly centers"; rumor; abandoned; bleak; remote; evacuation; commission; concluded; injustice; descent; prejudice; hysteria; political

For Discussion: How do the mailing address and the actual address differ? Who is Hermie? What were some of the reasons that Mama was upset? How did it feel to stand in line at a soup kitchen? Why did the camp feel like a prison? Why do you think only Japanese were placed in the camps even though the U.S. was at war with Germany and Italy, too? Explain why Jimbo thought that war makes people crazy. Do you agree or disagree? What luxuries were lacking at the camp?

Activities:

- Read the Bill of Rights to the Constitution of the United States. Find out what is meant by due process. Which rights were violated when people of Japanese ancestry were imprisoned in the United States? What are your feelings about the encampment of the Japanese?

- Review the parts of a friendly letter. Use the worksheet on page 30 to help you. Direct the students to write a response to Jimbo's letter. Remind them to keep in mind how they think Hermie would react to Jimbo's news.

- Examine the portrait on page 59 of *The Big Book for Peace*. Discuss the feelings conveyed in this picture. Talk about the possible media used to create the portrait. Pair the students and have them take turns modeling and drawing. Keep the materials to a minimum (use pencils for the drawings). Extend the lesson by learning more about portrait drawing using mixed media to reflect an artist's style. Pages 65 and 93 of Teacher Created Materials' *Masterpiece of the Month* (#018) contain appropriate lessons on this topic.

- Read other novels about this time period. Three excellent stories are *Hiroshima No Pika* by Toshi Maruki (Lothrop, Lee and Shepard, 1980); *Farewell to Manzanar* by Jeanne Wakatsuki Houston and James D. Houston (Bantam Books, 1973); *Sadako and the Thousand Paper Cranes* by Eleanor Coerr (Putnam, 1977).

Follow-Ups:

- Research World War II and the events that led up to it. Find out why the Japanese bombed Pearl Harbor, why the U.S. dropped atomic bombs on Hiroshima and Nagasaki, and how other nations became involved. Find out about the roles of F.D. Roosevelt and Truman as U.S. Presidents during the conflict. Complete the Day of Infamy worksheet on page 31.

- Read the *Diary of Anne Frank* (Pendulum Press, 1979) to find out about another kind of prison.

Friendly Letters

A friendly letter contains five basic parts. Each one is described below.

Heading: includes your address and the date, which are written in the upper right-hand corner of the letter.

Salutation: the greeting; begins with Dear followed by the name of the person being written to; followed by a comma.

Body: the main part of the friendly letter; contains the writer's information and ideas: skip a line and indent the first line of this (and all successive) paragraphs.

Closing: words that the writer uses to sign-off; first word is capitalized and whole closing is followed by a comma, e.g. With love, or Yours truly,

Signature: final part of the friendly letter; write your name beneath the closing.

Label each part of the friendly letter below. Then add your own paragraph on the lines provided.

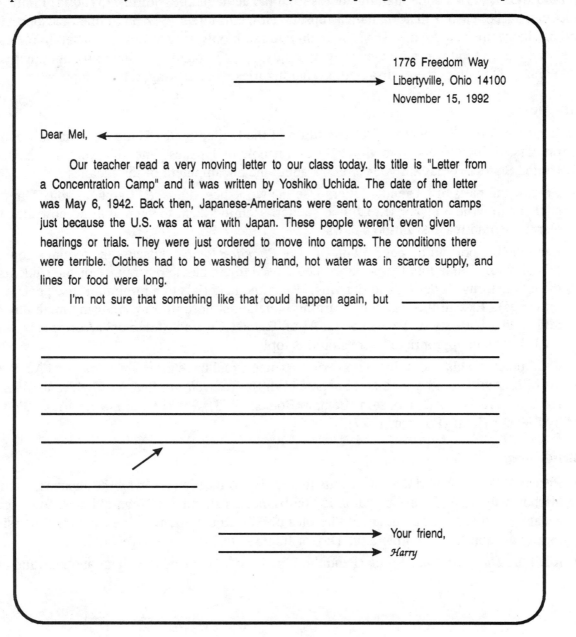

1776 Freedom Way
Libertyville, Ohio 14100
November 15, 1992

Dear Mel,

    Our teacher read a very moving letter to our class today. Its title is "Letter from a Concentration Camp" and it was written by Yoshiko Uchida. The date of the letter was May 6, 1942. Back then, Japanese-Americans were sent to concentration camps just because the U.S. was at war with Japan. These people weren't even given hearings or trials. They were just ordered to move into camps. The conditions there were terrible. Clothes had to be washed by hand, hot water was in scarce supply, and lines for food were long.

    I'm not sure that something like that could happen again, but _____

_____

_____

_____

_____

_____

Your friend,
Harry

Name _____

A Day of Infamy

After Japan launched a deliberate and unprovoked attack on Pearl Harbor, President Franklin Delano Roosevelt declared, "Yesterday, December 7, 1941 - a date which will live in infamy - the United States of America was suddenly and deliberately attacked by naval and air forces of the Empire of Japan." The Japanese all but destroyed the United States Navy. A large part of the Pacific Fleet had been based in Oahu - the island on which Pearl Harbor was located because it was considered to be safe. Unfortunately, the surprise invasion only pointed out how vulnerable or weak the island stations could be.

Two separate waves of planes about an hour apart dropped tons of bombs on targets throughout the island. Hundreds of planes were destroyed along with the huge battleships USS Shaw, USS Cassin, USS Pennsylvania, USS Downes, and USS Arizona. Countless human lives were lost. To honor the many men who sacrificed their lives that day a memorial, the USS Arizona Monument, was built over the sunken remains of that ship.

Learn more about Pearl Harbor Day as you label the map of Oahu, below, with the bolded names in each sentence.

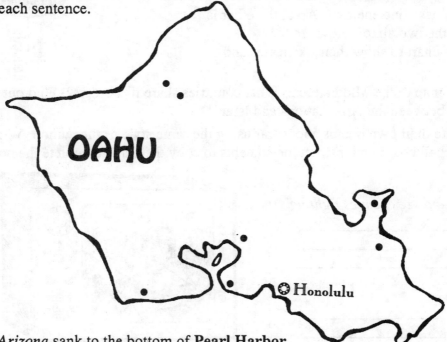

1. The *USS Arizona* sank to the bottom of **Pearl Harbor.**
2. At **Hickman Air Force Base** and **Bellows** and **Wheeler** air fields, most of the planes there were hit before they had time to get off the ground.
3. **Schofield Barracks** and **Kaneohe Naval Air Station** were severely damaged.
4. Hundreds of planes were destroyed at **Ewa Marine Corps Air Stations**.

On Your Own

- Find out the meaning of the battle cry, "Tora, tora, tora!"
- Make a list of the names of the battleships destroyed during the attack on Pearl Harbor.
- Who were the leaders of Japan and the United States at the time of the Pearl Harbor attack? Name some leaders of other countries at the time.

"Enemies"

by Charlotte Zolotow

Pre-Reading Activity: Have the students read *The Hating Book* by Charlotte Zolotow (Harper Row, 1969). Discuss moments of "unfriendship" that they may have experienced and how things were reconciled. Explain that they are now going to hear a poem about hate and enemies.

For Discussion: Who are the enemies? What images are shown on the TV? What is the answer to the two questions that end the poem? What is the author's message?

Activities:

- Draw the students' attention to the drawing on page 63 of *The Big Book for Peace*. What do they notice about the two figures? Have them make a list of the ways the two are alike.

- Brainstorm with the students some situations that might cause people to become enemies. Draw a web to illustrate these reasons.

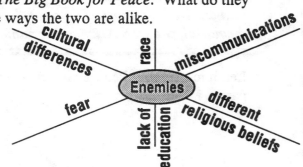

- In the poem "Enemies" one enemy is Arab, the other is Jewish. How are the two alike? How are they different? Make a chart to show their likenesses and differences.

- Locate Israel on a map of the Middle East. What countries share its borders? Find out the current status of relations between the Arab nations and Israel.

- Have students write their own poems about war using the same style as the author. Write the following on the chalkboard and instruct the students to copy them and complete the poem in their own words.

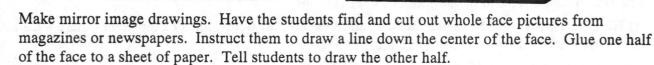

> *We watch TV and see enemies fighting.*
> *Close-ups of* _____
> _____
> _____
>
> *There are two.*
> *Which is* _____ ?
> *Which is* _____ ?

- Make mirror image drawings. Have the students find and cut out whole face pictures from magazines or newspapers. Instruct them to draw a line down the center of the face. Glue one half of the face to a sheet of paper. Tell students to draw the other half.

- Read other war poems. For example, "In Flanders Fields" by John McCrae; "War Is Kind" by Stephen Crane; "Conscientious Objector" by Edna St. Vincent Millay. All three can be found in *Peace and War* (see bibliography page 80).

Follow-Ups:

- Read the sentences on page 33. Substitute the bolded words with antonyms, or opposites. Compare the meaning of the sentences before the antonyms were added and after the antonyms have been added.

Name_____

A Day of Infamy

After Japan launched a deliberate and unprovoked attack on Pearl Harbor, President Franklin Delano Roosevelt declared, "Yesterday, December 7, 1941—a date which will live in infamy—the United States of America was suddenly and deliberately attacked by naval and air forces of the Empire of Japan." A large part of the United States Navy's Pacific Fleet had been based in Oahu—the island on which Pearl Harbor was located because it was considered to be safe. Unfortunately, the surprise invasion only pointed out how vulnerable or weak the island stations could be. Eighteen naval vessels in the harbor were destroyed.

Two separate waves of planes about an hour apart dropped tons of bombs on targets throughout the island. Almost two hundred planes were destroyed along with the huge battleships USS Shaw, USS Cassin, USS Pennsylvania, USS Downes, and USS Arizona. About 3,700 lives were lost. To honor the many men who sacrificed their lives that day a memorial, the USS Arizona Monument, was built over the sunken remains of that ship.

Learn more about Pearl Harbor Day as you label the map of Oahu, below, with the bolded names in each sentence.

1. The *USS Arizona* sank to the bottom of **Pearl Harbor**.
2. At **Hickman Air Force Base** and **Bellows** and **Wheeler** air fields, most of the planes there were hit before they had time to get off the ground.
3. **Scholfield Barracks** and **Kaneohe Naval Air Station** were severely damaged.
4. Many planes were destroyed at **Ewa Marine Corps Air Stations**.

On Your Own

- Find out the meaning of the battle cry, "Tora, tora, tora!"
- Make a list of the names of the battleships destroyed during the attack on Pearl Harbor.
- Who were the leaders of Japan and the United States at the time of the Pearl Harbor attack? Name some leaders of other countries at the time.

"The Bird's Peace"

by Jean Craighead George

Pre-Reading Activity: If possible, go on a walking tour to observe birds in action. Afterwards, discuss the birds' activities, where they were observed, how they communicated, etc. Did any of the birds appear to be fighting? Suggest that maybe they were trying to keep peace as they do in the story "The Bird's Peace."

Vocabulary: purling; lean-to; melodious; belligerent; sumac; thicket; incubating; serenely; preened; flicked; bracken; flitted; conspicuous; crouched; alighted; sapling; territory; brown-splotched

For Discussion: Why was Kristy upset? What caught her attention? Who were Fluter and Dulce? What was Dulce doing? How did Fluter protect her? What was Kristy's reaction to this scene? What were some of the fears that Kristy voiced? How were her fears answered? What had Kristy's father taught her about birds? What was Kristy able to teach her father about birds?

Activities:

- Finish Kristy's letter to her father. Begin it with, "Dear Daddy, I know how the birds keep the peace."

- Have a bird whistling contest to see who can sing the prettiest song. Make up a "stay-off-my-property" song and perform it for the class.

- Write a conversation that Fluter and the intruding sparrow might have if they could talk instead of sing.

- Create a cartoon strip to show the confrontation between Fluter and the other sparrow.

- Song sparrows have brown-splotched eggs. Research some other birds and find out what color eggs they lay. Make a chart to show this information.

- Write a report on sparrows. Work with a partner and brainstorm five different questions you have about sparrows. Research answers to the questions and write a report including all of the information gathered. Include illustrations to clarify main points. (See Writing a Report, page 57).

- Play a game of charades using words from the story. For example, act out a bird incubating her eggs or show a bird as it preens itself.

- Discuss how Kristy dealt with her fears in the story. How would you feel if someone you loved suddenly had to go to war? Who would you talk to? What would you do? With a partner, write a list of ways children could overcome and cope with a fearful situation.

- With a partner, make a web of story events. Put them in chronological order and then draw a picture of each one.

- What other lessons about peace can humans learn from animals? Write a story that tells how you or some other character learned a valuable lesson about peace from an animal.

Follow-Ups:

- Read Jean Craighead George's *One Day in the Tropical Rain Forest* (Crowell, 1990). Tell how the butterfly's existence contributed to peace.

- Make origami birds to symbolize peace doves. See page 35 for complete directions.

Peaceful Birds

Some birds represent peace. A dove is a symbol of peace all over the world. In Japan, the crane symbolizes the peaceful struggle of Sadako for life in *Sadako and the Thousand Paper Cranes*. Other countries honor different birds to symbolize peace. Students can make their own peaceful birds with the pattern below (or cut a 4-inch paper square) and the directions.

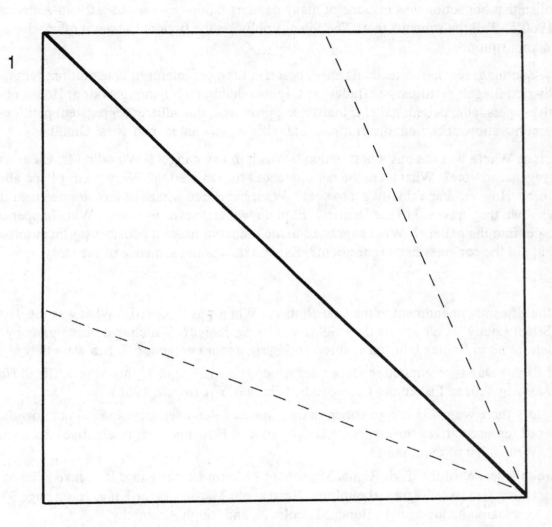

Directions:

* Cut out the square pattern. (1)

* Fold up on each dashed line to the bold center line. (2)

* Fold the small triangular corner up to the larger triangular top. (3)

* Fold down a tip of the small triangular corner. (4)

* Fold the whole figure in half towards the back. (5)

* Pull out the small triangle (beak) until the neck moves up. (6)

* Fold the feet out to the side.

* Draw eyes and other features.

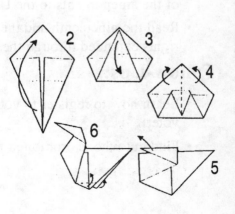

"The Silent Lobby"

by Mildred Pitts Walter

Pre-Reading Activity: Discuss Rosa Parks and the Montgomery bus boycott with the students. If you prefer, read selected segments from *Rosa Parks* by Greenfield (Thomas Y. Crowell, 1973) aloud to the class. Establish that her action was just one of many demonstrations by various African-Americans during the 1960's. Tell the students that "The Silent Lobby" is the fictional account of another nonviolent demonstration.

Vocabulary: soothing; register; intend; alarmed; poll tax; literacy; interpret; constitution; relief; represent; district; illegal; certificates; affadavits; Capitol; shabby; lobbying; gawking; House of Representatives; persuade; pelted; gallery; legislators; protested; threadbare; segregated; petitions; accounts; demonstrations; banning; discrimination; facilities; guarantee; penalties; Omnibus

For Discussion: Where was the bus's destination? Was it in any danger? Why did Mr. Clem warn Papa not to register to vote? What were the consequences for registering? Why wasn't Papa allowed to register to vote? How did Papa finally get to vote? What happened when the bus stopped near the Capitol? Why had they traveled to the District? Explain what it means to lobby. What happened when they tried to get into the gallery? What happened in the tunnel to make it possible for them to get passes? What did the congressmen argue about? Explain the ending sentence of the story.

Activities:

- Read the fifteenth amendment to the Constitution. When was it passed? What was the date of "The Silent Lobby"? Why were their rights still being denied? Which two bills signed by President Lyndon Baines Johnson ensured voting rights for everyone? When were they signed?

- Bill of Rights Day is celebrated in December which is also Human Rights Month. Read *Human Rights Day* by Aileen Fisher and Oliver Rabe (Thomas Y. Crowell, 1966).

- In the story there were 435 congressmen in the House of Representatives. Find out how the number of representatives for each state is determined. How many representatives does your state have? Write a list of their names.

- Research the leader of the Civil Rights Movement - Martin Luther King, Jr. Make a list of five new facts that you have learned about him. Read about Martin Luther King, Jr. on page 37. Others to research include Julian Bond, Malcolm X, and Ralph Abernathy.

- How well do you know your rights? Match the right with the amendment on page 38. Use a copy of the amendments to the U.S. Constitution to help you.

- Read the nineteenth and the twenty-sixth amendments to the Constitution. To whom were voting rights extended through these amendments? When were they passed?

Follow-Ups:

- Learn how to register to vote in your district. Find out the requirements to become a registered voter:

- Find out who is prohibited from voting. Practice voter registration with the form on page 39.

Name _____

About Martin Luther King, Jr.

Read the paragraphs about Martin Luther King, Jr. Answer the questions on the lines provided.

Civil Rights leader Dr. Martin Luther King, Jr. was born on January 15, 1929 in Atlanta, Georgia. He proved to be an excellent student, particularly in debate and public speaking. After graduating from Crozer Seminary, he went on to earn a doctorate from Boston University. While in Boston, he met Coretta Scott; they married on June 18, 1953. For five years Martin was pastor of Dexter Avenue Baptist Church in Montgomery, Alabama but in 1959 he resigned so that he could devote all his time to the civil rights cause.

King organized the Montgomery bus boycott in Montgomery, Alabama to force desegregation of the buses. He also led the Washington March of some 200,000 people in 1963. This demonstration led to the passage of the Civil Rights Act and Voting Rights Act in 1965. Later, he started the Poor People's Campaign to fight slum conditions in northern U.S. cities.

Dr. King's philosophy of civil disobedience and nonviolent protest echoed the beliefs of Mohandas Gandhi: "Attack the wrong, not the wrongdoer." In 1964 King was awarded the Nobel Peace Prize for his work for racial equality. Ironically, he died a violent death. On April 4, 1968 he was assassinated while at the Lorraine Motel in Memphis, Tennessee. Although his life ended abruptly and far before his work was done, Martin Luther King, Jr. left behind a legacy of hope in his now famous "I Have a Dream" speech.

1. Who was Martin Luther King, Jr.? _____

2. Name three nonviolent protests which he led.

    1. _____

    2. _____

    3. _____

3. What honor did King receive for his work? _____

4. What was King's philosophy? _____

5. On whose beliefs did Martin base his philosophy? _____

6. What did the Washington March accomplish? _____

    _____

7. How and when did Dr. King die? _____

8. What is the title of King's most famous speech? _____

Name _____

Know Your Rights

Draw a line from the stated right in Column I to its matching amendment in Column II. You may want to work with a partner on this assignment. Use a copy of the amendments to the U.S. Constitution to help you.

Column I	Column II
excessive bail shall not be required	XVI
prohibits slavery	I
limits a president to two terms in office	XXVI
guarantees freedom of speech, press, and religion	VII
guarantees women the right to vote	XVIII
gives the accused the right to a speedy, public trial	XIII
gives Congress the power to collect income tax	II
guarantees people of all races and color the right to vote	VIII
	V
people can keep and bear arms	VI
persons cannot be tried twice for the same offense	XIX
states may not abridge the privileges of U.S. citizens	IV
	XIV
prohibited the sale and manufacture of liquor	XXII
gives eighteen year olds the right to vote	XV
protects people against unreasonable search and seizure	
preserves the right of trial by jury	

Challenge: Write the Roman numerals I through X in a column. After each numeral explain the meaning of that amendment. Find out when the Bill of Rights were ratified.

Voter Registration

Before you can vote, you have to register with the Registrar of Voters. Usually that requires filling out a form and delivering it to the Office of the Registrar. Regulations vary from state to state; you may want to check with your local registrar for your specific requirements. The form below is just a sample of what might be used for voter registration. Pretend you are a U.S. citizen over the age of 18. Follow the directions on the form and fill it in completely. You may use your own name and address or make up the information.

Print in Ink	For U.S. Citizens Only
1 Name *(First Middle Last)*	**10** Have you ever registered to vote before? ○ Yes ○ No If yes, fill in with your most recent registration information.
2 Residence *(Number Street Apt. No.)*	Name, as registered.
City County Zip Code	Former Address
3 Mailing Address *(if different from residence)*	City County Zip
City State Zip Code	Political Party
4 Date of Birth **7** Occupation	Read this statement and warning before signing. *I am a citizen of the United States and will be at least 18 years of age at the time of the next election. I am not imprisoned or on parole for the conviction of a felony. I certify under penalty of perjury that the information on this affidavit is true and correct.*
5 Birthplace *(Name of U.S. State or Foreign Country)* **8** Telephone Area Code ( )	
6 Political Party *(check one)* **9** Optional Survey	**11** Signature: You **MUST** sign below.
☐ Democratic Party Can you help in the following?	
☐ Republican Party	_____ Signature
☐ Decline to State _____ Polling Place Worker	
☐ Other *(specify)* _____ Polling Site	_____ Date

"A Wild Safe Place"

by Maurice Sendak

Pre-Reading Activity: Students may already be familiar with the artwork and writing of Maurice Sendak. Share with students something about this prolific author/illustrator. A short biography follows.

> *Maurice Sendak was born June 10, 1928 in Brooklyn, New York. The youngest of three children, he was also the frailest, due to an early childhood bout with measles and pneumonia. Consequently, he was labeled sickly and found it difficult to make friends. Maurice was not particularly athletic, either; instead, he chose to stay home and draw.*
>
> *Mr. Sendak attended Art Students' League for two years and began working at various jobs. His first was working for a comic book syndicate. For three years he was a display artist for F.A.O. Schwartz. He also had some one-man exhibitions of his art.*
>
> *But it wasn't until he worked with author Ruth Krauss on* A Hole Is To Dig *that his reputation as a major children's book illustrator was established. Four years later in 1956 he wrote his first book,* Kenny's Window. Where the Wild Things Are, *created in 1963, stirred some controversy over its illustrations. Some librarians felt that the pictures were too scary for small children. However, Sendak answered his critics by explaining that the illustrations were a means for children to work through the fears and anxieties of everyday life. In 1964,* **Where the Wild Things Are** *was awarded the Caldecott Medal. Since then, Maurice Sendak has received many more awards and brought joy and imagination to countless readers the world over.*

Activities:

- Display the cover or page 83 of *The Big Book for Peace*. Discuss with students why they do or do not think "A Wild Safe Place" is an appropriate title. Talk about what it means to them. Have a copy of *Where The Wild Things Are* available for students to compare illustrations.

- Make giant wild, safe places. Pair the students. Have them take turns tracing around one another's body on a sheet of butcher paper. (One student lies on top of the butcher paper on the floor while the other student traces the outline with a black line marking pen). Cut out the shapes. Direct the students to decorate the shapes and add details. They may make a nest for the head or place it on an outstretched arm.

- Another wild safe place art project is a 3-dimensional collage. Divide the students into groups. Each group will need a basket or a paper bag (roll the edges of the top down about ⅓ of the bag). Fill the basket or bag with shredded tissue or newspaper. Draw, or cut out pictures from magazines, of people and animals who need a wild safe place to live.

- Write a story to go along with the picture. Give the monster a name and explain how the birds came to nest on his head.

Follow-Ups:

- Find and read some other Maurice Sendak books which contain monster illustrations.

"One More Time"

by Nancy Willard

Pre-Reading Activity: On the chalkboard or overhead projector write the words to the first verse of "One More Time." Direct the students to copy the words on a sheet of paper. Play the melody on the piano or the guitar. Repeat, this time singing the words to the melody. Have the students follow along on their word sheets.

Activities:

- Discuss the meaning of the words in the first stanza. Who is Captain Noah? Establish the Biblical story about Noah's ark and the ensuing flood.

- Learn the melody of "One More Time." Sing the words to the melody.

- Divide the students into small groups. Supply each group with a different verse to the song. Have them discuss and write what they think the verse means.

- Direct the students to write the words for a sixth verse. Pair the students for this activity. In a large group share the new verses.

- Display the picture on page 85 of *The Big Book for Peace*. Tell the students to make a list of everything they see in the picture. Which images refer to the words in the verses?

- Have the students make a collage to represent the verses. Divide the students into small groups. Supply each group with old magazines and newspapers, scissors, glue, and a sheet of cardboard (cut apart a large cereal box or other container). Tell the students to find pictures which represent words in the song. Cut out the images and arrange them on the cardboard. When everyone is satisfied with the arrangement, glue the pictures to the cardboard. Display the collages on the chalk tray or a classroom wall.

- Extend the collage activity with this idea. Number each collage. Direct the students to submit a name for each one. As a class, vote on names for each one. Note: It may be best to vote on a name for a different collage on separate days.

- Learn how to read music. For some this may be a review; for others it may be new information. A sheet of helpful music information can be found on page 42.

- Group the students in threes or fours. Direct the groups to write the words and music to a new song about peace. Have them record it on a tape player. Tell them to introduce and identify themselves on the tape before recording the song. Students can listen to the music during designated times at the classroom listening center.

- Record the entire class as they sing all five verses of "One More Time." (Use a video recorder if one is available.) Play it back and invite all students to critique the performance.

Follow-Ups:

- Learn the words and music to "Let There Be Peace on Earth." An easy arrangement can be found in *Brimhall Easy Piano Arrangements, Issue Number 4*. This book is available through music stores.

Musical Fact Sheet

This handy reference page will help you understand music and how it is written. Refer to the diagrams to help you as you read the text.

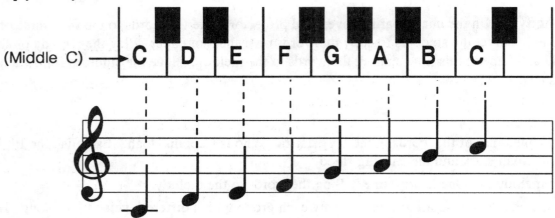

* Music is written on a staff which consists of five lines and four spaces.

* Each space and each line corresponds to a note on the piano keys (see diagram above).

* A treble clef is a sign written at the beginning of the staff. The treble clef indicates that the right hand plays these notes which are the melody.

* Music is divided into measures on the staff by bar lines.

* A double bar line appears at the end of a piece of music and indicates that the piece is done.

* A time sign tells about the timing of the music. The upper numeral means that there are four beats to each measure. The lower numeral says that a quarter note gets one beat.

* Whole notes are written o . Half notes are written ♩. Quarter notes are written ♩.

* In ⁴/₄ time, a whole note gets four beats per measure; each half note gets two beats per measure; and each quarter note gets one beat per measure.

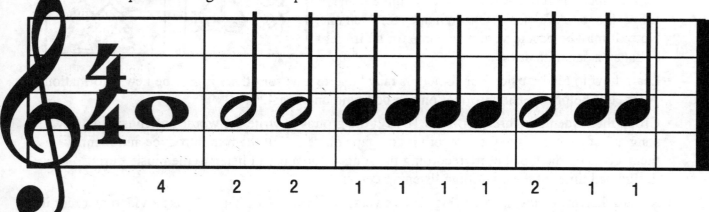

On Your Own:

* Find the notes in the top diagram on a piano.

* Look at some sheet music. Identify the time and the kind of notes used.

* Write a simple melody. Draw your own staff and notes.

* Explain how notes would be counted in ³/₄ time.

"I Was There"

by Marilyn Sachs

Pre-Reading Activity: Listen to and possibly sing some protest songs of the 1960's, for example "Blowin in the Wind" or "If I Had a Hammer" by Peter, Paul, and Mary; "Peace Train" by Cat Stevens; music by Joan Baez, Bob Dylan, and Arlo Guthrie. Explain to students that the 1960's was an era of change and protest; people were concerned about Civil Rights and the U.S. involvement in the Vietnam conflict. This selection, "I Was There," is also about protest and causes.

For Discussion: What causes were being protested? What causes were being supported? How old do you you think the narrator of this story is? What does that say about being involved in supporting a cause or protesting an event? Do you think it does any good to protest or fight for a cause? What are some ways causes were supported in the story? How was the end of the war celebrated?

Activities:

- Make a list of all the environmental, human rights, and political causes that you have ever heard of. Find out their addresses or phone numbers. Write or call one or more of them for further information. (Some agencies are listed in the book *50 Simple Things You Can Do To Save the Earth* by the Earthworks Group, EarthWorks Press, 1989.)

- Divide the students into small groups. Have each group research a cause that interests them. Tell them to create a banner that supports their cause. The banner should include how-to information plus the name and address of an appropriate agency which others can contract.

- With the class, brainstorm a list of ways that students could contribute to a specific cause. Make a web of the responses and save for future reference. Choose one or more of the methods for a whole class project; let the class vote on what they would like to do. Or, assign each group a different project. Have them devise a plan for implementing the project; present the plan to the whole class for discussion.

- Research the Civil Rights and the Vietnam protests of the 1960's. Specific topics include the Washington March of 1963 led by Dr. Martin Luther King, Jr. and the Kent State shooting in 1969.

- Find out about the Peace Corps. Under which president and when was it instituted? What is its purpose? Who can volunteer? Would you? Why or why not? (See page 64 for a look at the Peace Corps).

Follow-Ups:

- Read any of the books in the *Where Is Waldo?* series.

- Draw an "I Was There" picture similar to the picture on page 90 of *The Big Book for Peace* and any of the Waldo pictures.

- Learn about causes and effects; use the worksheet on page 44.

Name _____

Cause and Effect

Cause and effect refers to the relationship between events. When one thing happens other events may occur as a result. For example, the wind blows off your hat; this is the **cause**. As a result, your hair could get messed up or your ears might get cold. These are the **effects** or what happens when the wind blows off your hat.

Listed below are a number of causes. The box contains some effects of these causes. Find two effects for every cause and write them on the lines provided.

> * They tried to outdo one another.
> * Islanders gave up racing and wrestling.
> * He is ordered to stand for 36 hours.
> * Japanese-Americans were sent to camps.
> * Her friend said, "I hate you."
> * He is finally sentenced to death by a firing squad.
> * She became lonely and bored.
> * They knocked it down and built two castles.
> * Friends and relatives lost contact with one another.
> * People feared and distrusted Japanese-Americans.

1. Japan and the United States were engaged in war.

   a. _____

   b. _____

2. Two brothers inherited one castle.

   a. _____

   b. _____

3. Seth refused to join the Army.

   a. _____

   b. _____

4. Chrissy attached a "Keep Out" sign on her tree house.

   a. _____

   b. _____

5. The Russian government declared no one could cross the International Date Line.

   a. _____

   b. _____

6. Write your own cause and effects on the lines below.

Cause: _____

Effects:

   a. _____

   b. _____

"A Midnight Clear"

by Katherine Paterson

Pre-Reading Activity: Discuss homeless people with the students; include where and how they live in your community. Ask the students if they have ever talked with or befriended one of these persons. Explain that "A Midnight Clear" is the story of a boy who becomes friends with an elderly homeless woman.

Vocabulary: algebra; oozing; clattered; hysterical; hallucination; rinky-dink; escalator; smothered; mutt; stucco; dingy; crimson; receptacle; cocked; spurted; glittering; towering; slammer; pickpocket; streetwalkers; policies; jabbed; delinquent; grumped; humphed; salute; pouting; special; draft; complicated; enthusiasm; stray; sagged; dusk; offended; shield; hades; spasm; instinctively; corridor; pulpit; pews; slumped; squinted; sanctuary; nosed about; hoarsely; solitary

For Discussion: Describe the image that Jeff kept seeing. What was Jeff's memory about the Christmas when he was three? Describe the woman who spoke to Jeff. What did she do with the broken bottle? Why? What did she think about his visions? What did the reverend instruct Mrs. Dodson to do? How did Jeff feel about her by now? What did they do with the five dollars? How did the waitress get a tip? Why did Jeff give Mrs. Dodson his phone number? What happened after Mrs. Dodson phoned Jeff? How did Jeff help her?

Activities:

- Write an essay describing the changes in Jeff's attitude towards Rosie as the story progresses.

- The author uses a number of slang expressions throughout the story including "fruit basket" and "slammer." Think of some common slang terms used by you and your classmates. Work in groups to write a dictionary of slang terms.

- Draw a picture of Rosie based on her description in the story.

- What Christmas hymn is the title of this story taken from? Find this hymn in a songbook and read the words. Find the Christmas songs in which the words *peace on earth* and *heavenly peace* appear.

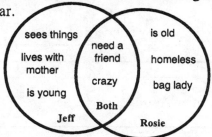

- Draw a cartoon of a child going to see Santa Claus for the first time. Write an appropriate caption.

- Construct a Venn diagram to show the likenesses and differences between Jeff and Rosie. Work with a partner to complete a diagram. If preferred, a chart of likenesses versus differences can be written instead of a Venn diagram.

- "Then, suddenly, she began to cough. Coughs that shook her whole body..." What do you think caused her cough? Research these diseases: tuberculosis, lung cancer, bronchitis, pneumonia. From which disease do you think Rosie was suffering?

Follow-Ups:

- Find out what is being done for the homeless people in your community. What do you think should be done to help them?

- Complete the Polar Opposites activity on page 46 as an oral exercise with the class.

Polar Opposites

One method of fostering critical thinking skills is an activity called polar opposites. This strategy involves rating characters and events in a story. It provides students with a concrete method of discussing these story elements. First, descriptive terms for a character or topic are rated on a scale of one to five. (A scale of one to five is more manageable than a scale with a higher outside number, but you may want to experiment with a scale of one to ten). The rating is then defended by using evidence from the story; life experiences can also be used to back up a choice. A sample polar opposite and its defense follow.

Jeff was a(n) _____ person.

1	2	3	4	5
inconsiderate				*considerate*

Five, for considerate, would be the likely choice in this case. Two events from the story that prove this are: 1) when Jeff breaks the beer bottle, he apologizes after Rosie yells at him 2) Jeff puts his jacket over Rosie's legs when she takes refuge in a church. (Other examples from "A Midnight Clear" could also be used.)

Model the above example by writing it on the chalkboard or overhead projector. Encourage the students to make a choice based on what they know and then have them find supporting evidence in the text.

Some other possible polar opposite topics are listed below. Be sure to complete each statement as a whole class and only work with one polar opposite at a time. Keep in mind that it is not as important that a "correct" number be chosen as it is that proper support can be supplied for a given choice. Once students are familiar with the process, have them create their own polar opposites examples for other literature selections.

1. Rosie is _____.

1	2	3	4	5
not crazy				*very crazy*

2. The reverend was _____ about Rosie.

1	2	3	4	5
not concerned				*very concerned*

3. Jeff is _____.

1	2	3	4	5
not afraid				*afraid*

4. Rosie's health is _____.

1	2	3	4	5
not good				*good*

5. Jeff's mother was _____.

1	2	3	4	5
hysterical				*very hysterical*

"A Ruckus"
by Thacher Hurd

Pre-Reading Activity: Display a copy of the Sunday comics. With the class, discuss which comics appeal most to them and why. Poll the class for their favorite cartoons. Explain that "A Ruckus" is a cartoon about peace.

Activities:

- Brainstorm some other captions for each page in "A Ruckus." Read the new story aloud.

- With the class discuss the message of "A Ruckus."

- Divide the students into small groups. Direct them to make their own cartoon story for the overhead projector. Have them use sheets of acetate and draw on them with fine line colored marking pens. When all the groups have completed their projects have one group at a time present their cartoon to the rest of the class.

- Tell the students to write a creative story about intergalactic peace. Write some suggested titles on the board: *The Ruckus on Mars; The Return of the Ruckus-Makers; How to Make a Peaceful Ruckus; How the Ruckus Brought Peace to Earth; A Year of Ruckuses.*

- Group the students. Tell them to create a song or a dance or both for peace on earth; present it to the class.

- Have the students draw a new design for a rocket.

- Make see-through murals depicting a ruckus for peace. Pair the students to work on one together. Materials and directions are below.

  Materials: clear adhesive paper; construction paper; crayons; colored markers; scissors; string; any or all of the following - art tissue, fabric scraps, colored acetate, wallpaper samples, wrapping paper, foil, yarn, magazines, newspaper, or any other appropriate material.

Directions:

- Cut out character shapes and other figures for the cartoon from the paper, fabric, foil, or any other materials gathered.

- With the marking pens write captions or a story on strips of construction paper.

- Cut two equal-size pieces from the roll of clear adhesive.

- Peel away the backing of one piece and reserve the other.

- Place the peeled sheet stick side up on a flat surface.

- Carefully arrange the figures and captions on the sticky surface.

- Peel away the backing of the reserved adhesive sheet.

- Carefully lay the adhesive sheet over the first sheet.

- Press the two sheets together to seal them securely.

- Display the finished murals from a clothesline strung safely across a wall.

Follow-Up:

- Create a cartoon with the figures on page 48.

- Learn about rockets. A sample worksheet can be found on page 61.

Cartoon Ruckus

Create a cartoon story using a similar style to that found in "A Ruckus." Color and cut out the characters and figures below. Arrange them on an 8 ½" x 11" (21 cm x 28 cm) sheet of index stock or construction paper. Glue the figures to the background when you are satisfied with the arrangement. Draw more details or cut out pictures from magazines to add to the background. Add cartoon bubbles and write captions in them.

Name _____

A Memory Test

Now that you have read *The Big Book for Peace* test your memory to see how well you remembered each story. In the space before each question write the number that corresponds to the correct title. Titles and their numbers can be found in the box below.

1. "The Dream"	7. "Law of the Great Peace"	13. "A Wild Safe Place"
2. "The Two Brothers"	8. "The Bus for Deadhorse"	14. "One More Time"
3. "There Is an Island"	9. "Letter From a Concentration Camp"	15. "I Was There"
4. "The Game"	10. "Enemies"	16. "A Midnight Clear"
5. "The Tree House"	11. "The Birds' Peace"	17. "A Ruckus"
6. "They That Take the Sword"	12. "The Silent Lobby"	

In which story...

1. _____ does a lone man stand up to the Army?

2. _____ were people unjustly imprisoned?

3. _____ do sparrows teach a girl about peace?

4. _____ do twins try to outdo one another?

5. _____ do birds live in a nest atop a monster's head?

6. _____ does a teenage boy befriend a homeless woman?

7. _____ do people petition the gods before a whale hunt?

8. _____ were five or six Native American tribes united?

9. _____ is a man denied the right to vote because of his color?

10. _____ are there no words?

11. _____ do plastic toy soldiers come to life?

12. _____ does a boy worry about his dog?

13. _____ do cartoon characters sing and dance for peace?

14. _____ do we watch war on television?

15. _____ does a giant straddle the Bering Sea?

16. _____ does a little girl protest cutting down trees in a park?

17. _____ do two girls put up signs that say "Keep Out"?

18. _____ does a busload of people travel from Mississippi to the Capitol?

19. _____ does a conflict arise over one castle?

20. _____ was there a peaceable kingdom?

21. _____ does a man enjoy his cat more than his children?

22. _____ does a man find the Quaker beliefs about slavery similar to his own?

23. _____ does a father have four spoiled children?

24. _____ are words set to music?

25. _____ does a boy see mushroom clouds?

Authors and Illustrators

The selected literature in *The Big Book for Peace* may elicit some student interest in a particular author or illustrator. Encourage and foster this interest through any of the following activities. Note: The last five ideas may be more appropriate for teachers than students.

❑ Learn about the author or illustrator by reading about them on the book jacket.

❑ For further information find any of the following reference books in the children's section of the local library.

    1. *Something About the Author* published by Gale Research and updated yearly.
    2. *The Illustrator's Notebook* published by The Horn Book, Incorporated, 1978.
    3. *Famous Children's Authors* published by T.S. Denison and Company, Incorporated.
    4. *Junior Authors and Illustrators* published H.W. Wilson Company.

❑ Scan the index of children's periodicals and educational journals to help find useful articles.

❑ Check the biography or autobiography shelves of the library. Samples include *Bill Peet: An Autobiography* (Houghton Mifflin, 1989) and *Laura Ingalls Wilder: Growing Up in the Little House* by Patricia Reilly Giff (Puffin, 1988).

❑ Write to the author or illustrator in care of the book publisher. This may or may not elicit a response due to the volumes of mail they receive.

❑ Find out about authors through book reviews in newspapers and community publications.

❑ Children's book stores often host children's authors and illustrators with a book-signing session; get a schedule so you can plan ahead to be there.

❑ Check out educational supply stores. They may stock, or have information about, books and anthologies of children's authors/illustrators.

❑ Take a class about children's literature. Check with colleges, universities, and other institutions which host community education services.

❑ Check with local colleges for special summer classes which feature children's authors.

❑ Look for notices about upcoming writer's conferences. Obtain a brochure and program of speakers. Often, they offer sessions by and about children's writers.

❑ Join a writer's club or attend a meeting when the hosted speaker is a children's book author.

Peace Word Banks

This resource page is a handy reference for various writing activities such as reports, creative writing, rhymes and poems, social studies lessons, and science experiments. In addition, these terms can be used for spelling words and vocabulary development.

Action Words

- negotiate
- talk
- discuss
- protest
- intervene
- pacify
- mediate
- listen
- agree
- disagree
- forgive
- pray
- advocate
- disarm
- demonstrate

Peace Symbols

- dove
- olive branch
- white flag

Peace Phrases

- peace, not war
- peaceful solution
- uneasy peace
- peace pipe
- peace offering

People To Know

Mohandas Gandhi	Mother Teresa	Alfred Nobel
Indira Gandhi	Mikhail Gorbachev	David Ben-Gurion
Martin Luther King, Jr.	Anwar El-Sadat	Chief Seattle
Coretta Scott King	Menachim Begin	Dag Hammarskjöld
Winnie Mandela	Dr. Maria Montessori	Rosa Parks
Nelson Mandela	Pope John XXIII	Albert Einstein
Desmond Tutu	Andrei Sakharov	Golda Meir
Jane Addams	Linus Pauling	Lech Walesa

Techniques

meditation	intervention	dialogue	marching
negotiation	pacifism	protesting	boycott
treaty	solidarity	prayer	disarmament
campaign	oratory	desegregate	sit-ins
amnesty	economic sanctions	diplomacy	conscientious objector

Terms

brotherhood	advocates	racism	rally
love	terrorism	militarism	slogan
détente	coalition	sexism	apartheid
peace	justice	activist	
conflict	equal	pacifist	
resolution	rights	global community	

Organizations

(See page 117 of *The Big Book for Peace* for five other organizations).

* Sierra Club 730 Polk Street San Francisco, CA 94109

* UNICEF 866 UN Plaza New York, NY 10017

* Peace Corps 1-800-424-8580

* Peace Corps Partnership Program 806 Connecticut Avenue, Northwest Room M-1210 Washington D.C., 20526

* United Nations UNA-USA Membership Department 485 Fifth Avenue New York, NY 10017-6104

Expanding Vocabulary

This page contains a number of fun ways for students to expand their vocabulary skills. For variety you may present an idea orally one time and then assign it in writing the next time. Some of these activities work just fine as homework assignments while others can be used as student assessment tools.

1. Write each vocabulary word on a separate index card or strip of construction paper. Divide the class into four or more teams. Give the first person on each team an equal number of random vocabulary words; place them face down on each desk. At a given signal they turn over the words and alphabetize them. When they are finished they may quietly stand up. As a class, review each participant's work. The first one to stand and alphabetize his/her words correctly earns 3 points for their team. All other correct word lists earn the team one point; no points are given for incorrect lists. Collect all the vocabulary cards, shuffle, and distribute to the next player in each team. Continue until all students have had a turn. The team with the highest score wins.

2. Prepare a list of vocabulary words on large, separate sticky notes. Randomly distribute the sticky notes. Ask all students with a vocabulary word beginning with A to stand. Tell them to determine as a group the correct alphabetical order of the words. Have them place the words in a column, one under the other (see illustration at right). Continue in the same manner until all words have been alphabetized. Note: You may want to write the first letter of the word above the column as shown in the illustration.

3. Recycle the sticky notes from exercise #2, above. Pair the students and have them alphabetize the whole list. As a follow-up, tell them to copy the alphabetized word list on a sheet of paper. Have the pair remove the sticky notes from the playing surface, in random order, and pass them on to another pair.

4. Recycle the index card or construction paper vocabulary cards from exercise #1 on this page. Give each student a card. Read aloud a definition of a word. The student with the word that has been defined stands up and shares his word with the class. You may ask students to use the words in an original sentence at that point. Note: If there are not enough vocabulary words in the given list, add to it or make duplicates of some words.

5. Assign each student a different vocabulary word. Direct them to define it, find a synonym and antonym for it, tell what part of speech it is, and learn its correct pronunciation. Then when you read a selection aloud to the students tell them to raise a hand when they first hear their word in the story. Ask them to define it, give an antonym, or tell what part of speech it is. They will want to be prepared for this oral activity!

Name _____

Make Peace Not War

A popular and much-quoted slogan during the 1960's protest rallies was "Make peace not war." Write your own alphabetical slogans by substituting other words for peace. An example is "Make apologies not war." The next statement in the list will replace *apologies* with a word that begins with the letter "B." For example, make brotherhood not war. Complete your alphabetical list on the lines below. Compare your completed list with a partner's.

A Make _____ not war.
B Make _____ not war.
C Make _____ not war.
D Make _____ not war.
E Make _____ not war.
F Make _____ not war.
G Make _____ not war.
H Make _____ not war.
I Make _____ not war.
J Make _____ not war.
K Make _____ not war.
L Make _____ not war.
M Make _____ not war.
N Make _____ not war.
O Make _____ not war.
P Make _____ not war.
Q Make _____ not war.
R Make _____ not war.
S Make _____ not war.
T Make _____ not war.
U Make _____ not war.
V Make _____ not war.
W Make _____ not war.
X Make _____ not war.
Y Make _____ not war.
Z Make _____ not war.

Challenge:

Work with a partner or a small group. Brainstorm an alphabetical list of war-related words, e.g. air raids, bombs, coup, etc. Begin each statement with, "Don't make_____, make peace." Write the statement twenty-six times replacing the blank each time with a different word from the alphabetical list.

An Abstraction

As you will recall, a noun is a word which is the name of a person, place, thing, or idea. Some examples of nouns include officer, field, newspaper, and peace. The words officer, field, and newspaper are examples of concrete nouns because they name something tangible; that is, they can be seen or touched. The word peace, however, is an abstract noun because it names something you can think about but that can neither be seen nor touched.

Read the sentences below and circle all the nouns. Then write the nouns in the proper section of the box at the bottom of this page.

1. *The Big Book for Peace* is a very special volume written by more than thirty authors and illustrators of children's books.

2. It contains stories, pictures, poems, and even a song.

3. Themes include peace, harmony, and understanding of various beliefs.

4. Story contents, range from humorous to fanciful to thought-provoking.

5. Most of all, it is a celebration of peace and hope for a peaceful world in the future.

Concrete	*Abstract*

Activities:

- Write a story using all the abstract nouns.
- Classify all the concrete and abstract nouns above as singular or plural; proper or common.
- Make a list of ten more abstract nouns.

Creative Writing

As the Peace thematic unit progresses, incorporate any of the following creative projects appropriate within your studies. For example, you may want to use the Peace Begins with Me writing idea as a follow-up to the reading of *Peace Begins with You* by Katherine Scholes. (Sierra Club Books, 1990). Other projects may be used as daily writing prompts or can become an ongoing activity to last the length of the unit.

* **Recipes for Peace.** Display the Recipe for Happiness from page 56. (Make an overhead transparency or copy it on the chalkboard or give each student a copy of that page.) List original ingredients and directions on large recipe cards or index cards, or cut off the bottom portion of page 56 and glue to heavy paper. Punch one hole in the top left corner of each card; strengthen with hole reinforcers (available at office supply stores). Make a cover, compile the cards behind it, and slip a metal clasp ring through the holes.

* **Peace Begins with Me.** Direct the students to rewrite the book *Peace Begins with You.* Brainstorm various methods they will employ in their daily lives to maintain peace among family members and school companions.

* **I Have a Dream.** Martin Luther King, Jr. had a dream that "...little black boys and black girls will be able to join hands with little white boys and white girls as sisters and brothers." Tell students to describe in writing their dreams for peace.

* **I Get Angry When...** With the class brainstorm situations that cause the students to become upset and angry. Have them write, "I get angry when..." five times on a sheet of paper leaving enough space between repetitions for completion. Direct the students to finish the phrase five different ways.

* **The Non-Quarreling Book.** Read aloud Charlotte Zolotow's *The Quarreling Book* (Harper & Row, 1963). Group the students and have them write an innovation of the story; title it *The Non-Quarreling Book.* Rewrite the quarrels so they are peaceful situations.

* **I Used to Think That.** On the chalkboard write the following incomplete sentence: I used to think that Peace_____ but now I know _____. Discuss possible ways to complete the sentence, e.g. I used to think Peace was none of my business but now I know I need to become involved. Direct the students to complete the phrase and write it on a strip of construction paper about the size of a bumper sticker. Display phrases on a wall.

* **Peace Journal.** Have the students begin a Peace Journal. Each morning direct them to write one thing they will do for peace that day. Right before dismissal for the day, have the students evaluate themselves by writing about what they did and explaining if it worked or failed.

* **Dear Abby.** Share with students a letter and its answer from an advice column in a newspaper or magazine. Direct the students to write their own questions about peace and address the letters to Dear Abby or another advice columnist. When all students have completed a letter, have them exchange their papers and write an answer to the question. Share the letters and their answers in small groups. Have each group choose one letter to share with the whole group.

Recipe for Happiness

Read the recipe for happiness which follows. Then on the lines provided write your own recipe for Peace.

Ingredients:

1 cup of freedom   1 ⅓ cups of helping others

4 teaspoons of fun   1 family

¼ cup of self-esteem   1 ½ cups of forgiveness

1 cup of honesty   1 whole pitcher of love

1 cup of understanding

Schoolwork, studies, and hobbies—as much as needed.

Directions:

Mix all the ingredients listed above until they are well-blended into a small body and mind. Store extra amounts in school, at home, and in neighborhoods, cities, and nations. Use daily for a lifetime of happiness.

Recipe for _____

Ingredients:

_____   _____

_____   _____

_____   _____

_____   _____

_____   _____

Directions:

_____

_____

_____

_____

_____

Writing a Report

Follow the steps in the flow chart below to help you write a report.

Choose a topic. Keep it specific. For example, Famous People is too general but Indira Gandhi is a specific famous person.

Write Five Questions About the Topic. For example, 1. Who was her famous family? 2. Where was she educated? 3. How did she become prime minister? 4. When and where was she born? 5. What did she accomplish during her lifetime?

Put the Questions in Good Order. For example, 4, 2, 1, 3, 5.

Do Research. Use a variety of books: Texts, biographies, encyclopedias, and other reference books. Write notes on index cards.

Write the Report. Write three or four sentences about each of the five questions. For example, (3). When India gained its independence, Indira's father became prime minister. She acted as official hostess since her mother had died years earlier. This political experience helped her become a strong leader.

Bibliography. At the end of your report write the title, author, and publishing information of each book researched. For example, Church, Carol Bauer. *Indira Gandhi, Rose of India.* Greenhaven Press, Incorporated, 1976.

END

Listed below are some possible research topics. Some may need to be made more specific.

* Earth Day	* David Ben-Gurion	* Peace
* Civil Rights	* Chief Seattle	* War
* Attack on Pearl Harbor	* Anwar El-Sadat	* Unicef
* *The USS Arizona*	* Dag Hammarskjöld	* Greenpeace
* Apartheid	* Mikhail Gorbachev	* Rain forests
* Nobel Peace Prize	* Nelson Mandela	* The environment
* The United States	* Dr. Maria Montessori	* Native Americans
* Homeless people	* Coretta Scott King	* Black History
* World War II	* Mother Teresa	* Glasnost
* Vietnam conflict	* Rosa Parks	* Development of Atomic Bomb

Math Lessons

Incorporating math into your Peace unit may present a challenge, but there are methods that can be used without a lot of advance preparation. Some sample ideas follow to help you create your own ideas.

Mathematical Vocabulary. Tell the students to divide all the vocabulary words into syllables and find the average number of syllables per word. Write the vocabulary/spelling words in expanded notation. For example, petition = pe+ti+tion. Make fractions from the words: pe|ti|tion or (petition circle graphic)

Map Strategies. Anytime maps are used, direct students to measure the distances between two locations using a length of string and the map's scale. Have the students estimate distances before actually measuring.

- Compare measurements made on a flat map and a globe. Challenge students to find the distance from the two farthest points on a particular map. For example, find the distance between the two farthest cities in North Dakota or Mississippi.

Popularity Polls. After a particular selection, poll the students with questions such as these: How many thought the solution was fair and equitable? How many liked the ending? How many would have acted differently if they were the main character? Graph the results. Break the results into boys versus girls and re-graph the results. Make a living graph. Ask students a question that has three choices for answers. Give each student a sticky note

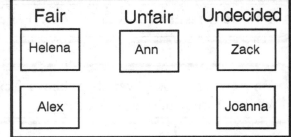

Fair	Unfair	Undecided
Helena	Ann	Zack
Alex		Joanna

on which to indicate a choice. Write appropriate headings on the chalkboard. One at a time have the students place their choices under the proper heading; you may want them to verbalize the reason for the choice. Use the information gathered to write fractions and/or percentages. For example if twelve students out of thirty chose answer A, what fractions is that? ($^{12}/_{30}$). Reduce it to lowest terms. ($^2/_5$). Convert that to a percentage. (2 + 5= .40 or 40%, or $^2/_5 = {}^{40}/_{100}$).

- Compose word problems about the information gathered. For example, if eight students chose answer A, how many chose another answer? What is the difference between the number of students who chose answer C and the number who chose answer B?

Secret Codes. Review basic math facts with this strategy. First, arbitrarily assign a value to each letter of the alphabet and write the letters and their corresponding values on the chalkboard or overhead projector. Pose a question to the students, for example, what world leader is famous for encouraging civil disobedience? On the chalkboard draw the appropriate number of spaces for the answer; in this case Gandhi requires six spaces (see illustration at left). Below each line write a problem that corresponds with the letter value you have previously determined. For example, if you have assigned A to be 49, then you must write a problem in which the answer is 49: 7x7, 40+9, 58-9, (6x5)+19, (100 +2)-1, etc. Write other questions and answers using the the same key.

Research. Assign students to research related facts. For example, after reading "They That Take the Sword" tell students to find out how many Confederates were wounded and killed as compared to how many Union soldiers were wounded and killed. Write the numerals in words (3,170 = three thousand one hundred seventy); expanded notation (3,170 = 3000+100+70+0); or create charts and graphs with the statistics.

Nobels for Peace

All five people below have these three things in common: They lived sometime during the 20th century, they worked for peace, and their peaceful efforts were awarded the Nobel Peace Prize. To figure out their names, use the coordinates below each line to find the letter in the grid. For example, (5,8) is J. (To find (5,8) start at 0 and move 5 spaces along the horizontal line; from there, count up 8 spaces on the vertical line. The letter at that point is a J.) Write the letter on the line above the corresponding coordinates. Continue to find the remaining letters in the same manner.

1. ___ ___ ___ ___ ___ ___ ___ ___ ___ ___
  (5,8) (4,10) (12,2) (2,7) (15,12) (18,4) (9,14) (10,1) (16, 11) (4,4)

2. ___ ___ ___ ___ ___ ___ ___ ___ ___ ___ ___
  (7,5) (10,12) (11,8) (20,2) (14,9) (19,7) (8,11) (20,15) (6,13) (1,11) (13,12)

3. Andrei ___ ___ ___ ___ ___ ___ ___ ___
  (2,14) (6,2) (15,5) (4,13) (19,5) (18,13) (20,11) (12,14)

4. ___ ___ ___ ___ ___ ___ ___ ___ ___ ___
  (8,9) (9,6) (5,15) (11,10) (8,8) (6,11) (16,7) (14,3) (17,14) (3,15)

5. Linus ___ ___ ___ ___ ___ ___ ___
  (1,4) (1,9) (3,2) (18,10) (10,3) (17,6) (5,12)

15	X	A	L	C	J	X	M	J	D	H	G	K	L	M	Z	Y	H	J	T
14	F	S	E	N	M	V	I	E	D	S	M	V	L	D	H	E	S	L	X	G
13	R	Q	D	H	P	U	W	H	R	L	J	K	W	K	L	C	Z	R	H	J
12	G	N	G	M	G	M	H	J	Q	E	G	J	U	M	A	I	H	I	D	E
11	T	W	I	O	Q	A	C	D	K	J	K	D	M	B	K	M	I	J	I	O
10	Q	B	F	A	O	I	Y	G	P	D	H	L	G	X	I	K	M	L	L	H
9	A	R	J	C	L	V	R	L	H	I	P	F	V	O	L	L	G	M	G	L
8	N	O	H	P	J	F	L	W	P	M	S	J	Z	C	G	D	J	K	K	F
7	O	E	C	G	D	H	C	I	L	H	L	M	J	I	N	L	K	D	N	M
6	B	S	K	H	J	L	M	R	E	K	O	Z	T	A	J	R	N	D	M	I
5	A	D	B	J	G	T	D	K	I	R	F	P	I	Z	K	J	C	P	A	K
4	P	U	L	S	I	K	S	D	M	S	V	I	T	F	P	D	L	D	S	C
3	C	W	P	A	K	S	L	F	I	L	R	W	E	D	M	G	S	F	O
2	G	D	U	K	R	A	Z	V	Z	T	M	N	U	K	Y	F	E	C	V	M
1	F	V	M	I	N	G	T	W	X	A	I	S	X	F	L	S	Y	O	C	F
0	1	2	3	4	5	6	7	8	9	10	11	12	13	14	15	16	17	18	19	20

Challenge: Find out more about each of the Nobel Prize winners above. Use an encyclopedia to help you. Another good resource is the book *The Peace Seekers, the Nobel Peace Prize* by Nathan Aaseng (Lerner Publications Company, 1987).

Hidden Peaceful Picture

To find the hidden picture on the dot matrix below solve each math problem. When you solve a problem find its answer on the matrix. For example, the answer to (9x3)+40 is 67. Locate 67 by counting over six more spaces from 61 (61+6=67). If the answer to the next problem was 84, you would count over three more from 81 (81+3=84) and connect that dot with the dot from the previous answer. Connect the dots in the same order that the problems appear.

1. (72+9)-2= _____

2. (40+5)-3= _____

3. (6x2)+2= _____

4. (48+12)+20= _____

5. (16x2)+1= _____

6. (9x3)+15= _____

7. (80+4)+32= _____

8. (15x4)+2= _____

9. (30x3)-18= _____

10. (25x3)+7= _____

11. (45x2)-7= _____

12. (60+3)+64= _____

13. (5x10)+25= _____

14. (70+2)+31= _____

15. (12x4)-1= _____

16. (4x8)+5= _____

17. (5x11)-29= _____

18. (40+2)-4= _____

Connect these dots:

19. (36x2)+20= _____

20. (12x6)+12)= _____

21. (35x2)+6= _____

22. (50+5)+58= _____

23. (100+2)+10= _____

Name _____

Rocketry

In 1914 when Robert Hutchings Goddard published articles about the multi-stage rocket he had patented, the scientific community paid little attention to his findings. One country, however, did take note of his research—Germany. The Germans built V-2 rockets based on Goddard's principle and launched these rockets in attacks against London during World War II. About the same time, Goddard began working for the United States Navy where he continued to develop weapons until his death in 1945. The applications of his work were not fully realized until some years later. Today, rockets are used to launch spacecraft into orbit, making the world a smaller, more united place to live. They burn liquid fuels and can operate in the vacuum of outerspace just as Goddard proved. Thanks to Robert Goddard, man's ability to explore the universe is a reality.

The diagram below shows the main parts of a modern rocket. Unscramble the letter groups beside each part and correctly write the name on the space provided.

Saturn V

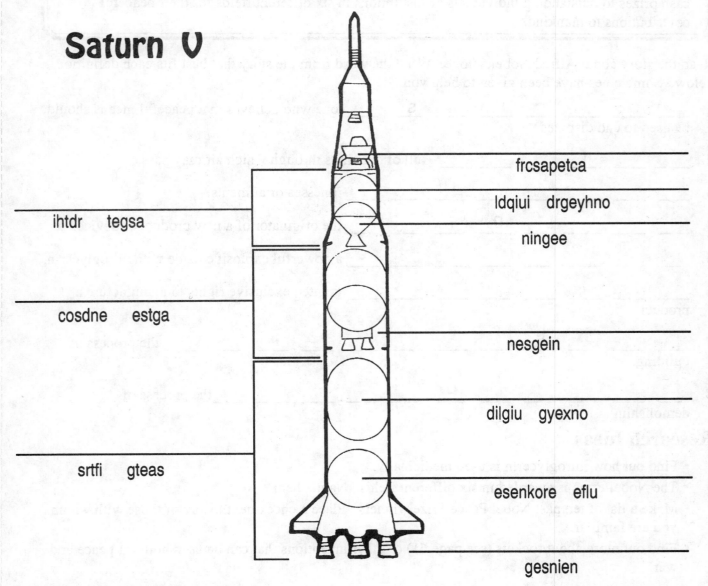

ihtdr   tegsa

cosdne   estga

srtfi   gteas

frcsapetca

ldqiui   drgeyhno

ningee

nesgein

dilgiu   gyexno

esenkore   eflu

gesnien

Construction Not Destruction

Alfred Bernard Nobel was the Swedish-born inventor of dynamite and other explosives. Born on October 21, 1833 in Stockholm, Nobel suffered from a variety of ailments including a weak heart. Because of these maladies he often missed school and would spend his hours at home drawing mechanical devices. Despite the missed days, Alfred was an A-student.

Later, he followed in his father's footsteps and began working with explosives. Nobel experimented with nitroglycerin as an aid in construction. However, it proved to be unstable and shock-sensitive. An accident with the substance killed his younger brother. Adjustments were made by absorbing the nitroglycerin in porous clay. The resulting product was just as powerful but could be handled safely. It was patented under the name dynamite.

Nobel, a life-long pacifist, intended for his invention to be used only for peaceful purposes. He was bitterly disappointed by the military use of his products and felt responsible for the destruction they caused. Before his death in 1896 he set aside the majority of his fortune in a trust fund and established the Nobel Foundation. This organization continues today to award cash prizes to outstanding individuals or institutions in six different fields for their peaceful contributions to mankind.

Read the story about Alfred Nobel, above. Write the word from the story that best fits each definition below. Some clues have been given to help you.

1. ___ ___ ___ ___ ___ ___ s ___ one who believes that peaceful means should be used to end disputes.

2. ___ ___ r ___ ___ ___ full of openings through which air may pass.

3. ___ ___ ___ ___ ___ i ___ ___ illnesses or ailments.

4. ___ ___ ___ ___ n ___ ___ ___ the originator of a new product or device.

5. ___ ___ ___ ___ ___ ___ e a powerful explosive made with nitroglycerin.

6. ___ ___ t ___ ___ ___ ___ ___ granted exclusive rights to manufacture a product.

7. ___ ___ ___ s ___ ___ ___ ___ ___ ___ ___ the process of building.

8. ___ ___ ___ ___ ___ u ___ ___ ___ ___ ___ the process of demolishing.

Research Ideas

- Find out how nitroglycerin is used medicinally.
- The Nobel Prize is awarded in six different fields. Name them.
- Make a list of ten past Nobel Peace Prize winners. Place a check next to any of those with whom you are familiar.
- Find out more about rockets (see page 61) or other inventions that can be used both for peace and war.

Peace Symbols

Some common peace symbols are depicted below. Use for student reference. You may want to enlarge the graphics with an overhead projector or at a copy store. These pictures can also be used for clip art on stationery, letters home, etc.

Bertrand Russell is credited with developing this Peace Symbol which was popularized during the protest of the Vietnam conflict in the late 1960's and early 1970's.

A white flag represents a truce to fighting.

The dove is accepted as a universal peace symbol.

V'd fingers mean peace, love, and harmony.

Olive branches symbolize peace.

Learn more about symbols. Read *Saying It Without Words* by Arnulf K. and Louise A. Esterer (Julian Messner, 1980).

A Look at the Peace Corps

The concept of a "peace corps" was first introduced to Congress in early 1960 but the bill failed. Not until presidential hopeful John F. Kennedy challenged University of Michigan students to work for freedom in other countries did the idea catch on. When Kennedy was elected president, the Peace Corps was official founded.

Today, over 100,000 volunteers have served in 91 different countries as ambassadors of peace. They have performed a variety of skills and services including teaching reading, teaching beekeeping, planting trees, helping sell handicrafts made by the villagers, teaching sign language to deaf children and adults, writing newsletters, and building ponds so people can have fish to eat.

To qualify for the Peace Corps you must be: 18 years of age or older; a United States citizen; in good health; and willing to serve for two years. You will be trained in the local language, beliefs, and values of your assigned country. Housing, food, travel, and medical expenses will be taken care of but you will not receive a salary. Instead, a readjustment allowance will be given to you when your service is completed.

If this sounds like something you would like to do, consider the following. You must be willing to learn another language, leave most of your possessions behind, eat new foods, and possibly live in a mud hut. There will be no television for entertainment, no hot baths, and no daily phone conversations with friends and family. The countries served by the Peace Corps are very poor and they lack even the basic facilities that we are accustomed to having and using.

Despite all these hardships many people continue to meet the challenge of the Peace Corps because they realize the importance of their contributions to help others. As recruitment advertisements said, the Peace Corps is the toughest job you'll ever love.

If you think you might be interested in becoming a Peace Corps volunteer, prepare for serving in the program by trying some of these activities.

1. When you become a teenager plan to live abroad with a host family through a student exchange program. For information write to Youth for Understanding, International Youth Exchange, 3501 Newark Street, Northwest, Washington, D.C. 20016 or President's International Youth Exchange, Pueblo, Colorado 81009.

2. The Girl Scouts offers International Wider Opportunities for its Cadettes and Seniors. Contact Girl Scouts of the USA, 830 Third Avenue, New York, New York 10022.

3. Participate in sports competition. Find out about Olympic Youth Camps from AAU/USA Junior Olympics, 3400 West 86th Street, Indianapolis, Indiana 46268.

4. Learn another language, take courses about world cultures, and read about other countries. Become involved through Save the Children Federation, Incorporated, 54 Wilton Road, Westport, Connecticut 06880.

5. Correspond with a pen pal in another country. For names and information write to International Pen Pals, P.O. Box 65, Brooklyn, New York 11229.

6. Help other people. Donate your services to a food bank, help at a community soup kitchen, or volunteer as a Red Cross aide.

7. Develop hobbies and interests - learn sign language, knitting, the law, etc.

8. Befriend foreign students at your school.

9. Read *The Peace Corps Today*. (See bibliography, page 80, for more information.)

A Worldwide Ruckus

Expand student awareness and knowledge of other peoples by having them come together and create a Worldwide Ruckus for Peace with this culminating event. Plan the activities and lessons well in advance of the estimated date of your Worldwide Ruckus so you will be ready to share your studies with schoolmates, parents, and community guests. Planning steps have been outlined for you below. All lessons and activities are suggestions that you will need to modify and adapt to fit your classroom needs.

Planning

1. Group activities into four different subject areas; 1) Social Studies/Geography; 2)Math/Science; 3)Language/Creative Writing; 4)Music/Art. Specific ideas for each area are presented below and on page 66 and 67.
2. Divide the students into small groups. Determine a country for each group to study (assign one or give them a choice from a prewritten list).
3. Once the countries have been assigned, present the activities. Give the groups a choice of two out of three activities from each subject area, for example.
4. Set aside a block of time each day to work on the projects.
5. Enlist volunteers to provide refreshments.
6. Plan the program for the Worldwide Ruckus day. (See sample program on page 68).
7. Make your own instruments for the parade (See page 69 for directions).
8. Begin rehearsing the events - the introductory speech, the parade, and the medley of songs.
9. One week before the event make and send invitations to other classes in the school, parents, and community guests. (See sample invitations on page 67.)
10. The day prior to the event check all groups to confirm necessary supplies. Also, set up the four display centers.
11. The day of the event recheck the displays, set up the refreshment center, and rehearse one last time.
12. Showtime!

Activities

Social Studies/Geography

- **Shape Reports**. Give each group a legal size (14 ³/₄" x 10"/ 37.5cm x 25.4cm) manila file folder, drawing paper, scissors, glue, and a marking pen. Direct them to draw an outline of their country, in pencil first, on the drawing paper. Reinforce the outline with the marking pen and cut it out. Glue to the front of the file folder. When it is dry, cut around the shape leaving part of the left, hinged side of the file folder intact so that it can be opened like a book. (Note: Students may draw directly onto the file folder if preferred. Also, students who are not comfortable with free hand drawing may want to trace a map). Open up the shape file folder. Have the students draw important physical features on the right inside page. The following features should be drawn and labeled: major rivers and other large bodies of water; mountain ranges; deserts; important cities; site of important man-made or natural structures; boundary lines between states or provinces; names of states or provinces. On the opposite inside page of the file folder write descriptions and statistics about these physical features. For example, India's Himalaya Mountains are the highest in the world. Its capital is New Delhi and is home to approximately 7.2 million people. Finally, on the back page tell the students to list information about population, language, religion, size, location, neighboring countries, government, etc. An almanac is an essential reference tool for this activity.

A Worldwide Ruckus (cont.)

Activities (cont.)

Social Studies/Geography (cont.)

- **Imports**. Have the students check the labels on clothing, toys, knicknacks, equipment and furnishings in their home (a great homework assignment). Tell them to write a list of the items and their country of origin. In a whole group begin a chart of imports by listing the countries being studied. Below each country write the items from the various countries that students have in their homes. Display the chart prominently and add to it throughout your studies. Set aside a day for students to bring in an actual import item to share with the class. Plan a field trip to an import store; assign students to write a list of ten unusual imports each from a different country.

- **Cultures**. Have the students learn something about the culture of their assigned country. Sample activities include reports on famous people, learning some words and sentences in a foreign language, comparing the roles of men and women in that society, finding out the type of government and the name of the current leader.

Math/Science

- **Currency**. First, tell the students to find out the name of the currency of their assigned country and its value. For example, India uses the rupee; approximately 17.5 rupee equal one American dollar. Compile a class chart of the information and keep the chart displayed prominently. Quiz the students about the values, e.g., Which country's currency is worth the most? Least? What is the difference between the two? Are any of the countries' currencies almost equal in value? Direct the groups to make line or bar graphs using the information from the chart. Bring in samples of foreign coins and currency.

  Currency Values

Country	Currency	Value per U.S. $1
India	rupee	17.5 = $1
Paraguay	guarani	1,213 = $1

- **Weather**. Explore how weather conditions have affected the various countries. The Thar Desert, for example, can be found in the northwestern section of India. It is an area of very little rainfall and temperature extremes. Find out what kind of plants and animals can survive in that environment, what crops can be grown there, how people dress, type of shelter used. See page 71 for some weather experiments.

- **Biomes**. The broad wildlife zones that cross the world are known as biomes; each climate houses a different variety of animals. The diagram at the right illustrates the different climate zones of the world. Have each group determine the biome(s) of their assigned country and research the animals that inhabit the region. Write the names of the animals in the proper section of the chart on page 72.

  Arctic
  Northern Temperate
  Northern Subtropical
  Tropical
  Southern Subtropical
  Southern Temperate
  Antarctic

Language/Creative Writing

- **Folk Tales.** Read some folktales from the countries being studied. A great resource for this activity is the book *Best-Loved Folk Tales of the World* selected by Joanna Cole (Doubleday, 1982). Have each group create an original folk tale for their country; draw pictures to go with the story. The groups may also want to write a prequel or sequel for a specific folk tale.

A Worldwide Ruckus *(cont.)*

Activities *(cont.)*

Language/Creative Writing *(cont.)*

- **A Play.** As a class write a play based on "A Ruckus" by Thacher Hurd in *The Big Book for Peace.* Create a cast of characters, the action, and complete dialogue. Choose a song to sing or form a band and make your own instruments. (For directions on making instruments see page 69). Determine what props will be needed and build them.

- **International Dictionary.** Begin an international dictionary that can be added to throughout the year. Direct each group to compile a list of foreign words that originate from their assigned country. Write each word and its definition on a separate index card as shown at left. Label the upper right corner with the country of origin. Alphabetize the words and place them in an index card file box. This can be an ongoing project throughout the year.

Music/Art.

- **Listen**. While students are completing seat work or reading, play traditional music from the various countries. Afterwords, discuss the origin of the music. Have the students identify any instruments they hear.

- **Learn the words and music to some traditional tunes.** Simple arrangements for the piano and electronic piano can be found in *The Usborne Book of Easy Piano Tunes* by Phillip Hawthorne (Usborne Publishing, 1989). Invite guests who may be able to perform traditional music or teach the students about an instrument. Make musical instruments (see page 69).

- **Art**. Visit a museum. Look in art books. Choose an activity from *The Metropolitan Museum of Art Activity Book* by Osa Brown (The Metropolitan Museum of Art, 1983). Make face masks that represent the traditional garb or a famous person from that country. For example, a Ghandi face may require a skull cap or skin-colored bathing cap. To make the mask, staple a tongue depressor to the bottom of a white paper plate. Hold the stick and place the mask in front of your face. Locate the eyes and lightly mark the spots with pencil. Cut out eye holes. Draw details— furrowed brow, mustache, etc. To complete the look drape a white sheet over one shoulder.

Making Invitations

- Use Teacher Created Materials' Earth Shape Note Pad (TCM 755) for your invitations to your classroom program. As a class (or within the assigned groups) compose the message of your invitation. A sample follows, or you may use the forms on page 70.

Dear Parents,
Please join our class in a Worldwide Ruckus for Peace at 2 p.m. on Friday, April 20. You will learn why we believe peace is important. You'll be treated to a play, learning centers, and refreshments. Join us!

Yours truly,
Linn Reid

Sample Checklist and Program

The following list is a sample of things that may need to be organized for your classroom program. Modify the checklist to reflect your own organization and schedule. The sample program at the bottom of the page is an example only. A final program should reflect the actual events of your worldwide ruckus.

Sample Checklist

✔ = completed   X = re-check

_____   Prepare lessons, worksheets, and gather necessary supplies for the activities.

_____   Divide students into groups; make master list of students in each group.

_____   Assign each group a different country for their studies.

_____   Present the projects, deadlines, and create a timetable.

_____   Enlist parent or other volunteers to provide refreshments.

_____   Plan the program for the Worldwide Ruckus.

_____   Make musical instruments.

_____   Rehearse the music and parade.

_____   Compose a guest list.

_____   Make invitations; check off names on guest list.

_____   Send invitations.

_____   Meet with each group to check its projects.

_____   Set up the four display centers.

_____   Dress rehearsal.

_____   Re-check the displays.

_____   Set up the refreshment center.

_____   Run through the sequence of events in the program.

_____   _____

Sample Program

A Worldwide Ruckus for Peace.
Presented by Mr. Cole's Sixth Grade Class.
On this 20th day of April, 19_____ .

2:00 p.m.	Welcome by Mr. Cole.
2:05 p.m.	Introduction and Purpose
	A Worldwide Ruckus Parade
	A Medley of Peace Songs
2:30-3:00	View the Centers
	Sample the Refreshments

Make copies of your final program for all guests or make one giant poster with the events listed and post it so it is highly visible.

Instruments for a Ruckus

It is fitting that a Ruckus for Peace should include some type of noisemakers. A bunch of fun ideas appear below but don't limit your sounds to these instruments - invent some of your own.

Musical Rulers

Place a plastic or wood ruler flat on a table. Hold the ruler so that half of it sticks out over the edge. With your other hand pluck the hanging end of the ruler. Move more of the ruler onto the table; listen to the sound made when it is plucked now.

Pop Xylophone

You will need four or more same-size empty soda pop bottles, water, and a wooden spoon. Arrange the bottles side by side on a flat surface. Fill each bottle with a different amount of water starting with the most water on the left down to almost no water on the right (see diagram). Tap the side of each bottle with the spoon. Create a melody of your own.

Tissue Box Guitar

Attach two wood dowels or blocks on either side of the hole of a tissue box. Stretch several rubber bands of varying lengths and thicknesses across the top and around the perimeter of the tissue box (see diagram). Strum strings with your fingers or use a plastic bread wrapper for a pick.

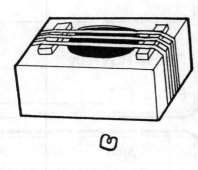

Reeds

To make a reed instrument cut a piece of old garden hose into a three foot (1m) length. Practice blowing into the top of the reed by pressing your lips tightly and then less tightly together. Another reed can be made by flattening one end of a straw and cutting a V onto that end. Hold the cut end lightly between your lips as you blow.

Rattlers

Fill empty plastic margarine tubs or yogurt cups with paper clips, buttons, marbles, dried beans, rice, even pushpins. Attach the lid and shake it up. Experiment with the items by putting only one kind in some cups and mixing up the contents of other cups.

Screechers

Blow up a balloon. Pinch the neck of the balloon with the first fingers and thumbs of each hand on either side. Slowly pull apart the sides of neck. As air is released, sounds will be made.

Drums

Use empty plastic bowls or cardboard boxes to make drums. Cut a plastic bag open and stretch it across the bowl or open end of the box. Have a partner tie string around the edge as you pull the plastic bag tightly. Tape the plastic in place. Play the drum with your fingers or a pencil.

A Worldwide Ruckus Invitation

Dear _____,

The _____ grade class in Room _____ of _____
         Level   *Number*   *School Name*
School under the supervision of_____
                                        Teacher's Name
has prepared a peaceful demonstration for you to share.
Come learn why we think PEACE is so important and how we are trying to
spread the message of PEACE.
Please join us at _____ sharp on _____
                        Time   *Day*
_____ for a learning experience you won't want to miss!
      Date

From

_____
         Signature

Please RSVP by _____
                        Date
Phone (   ) _____

Spain   Italy   Korea   India   Canada   Mexico   Germany   Greenland

Cuba   Dear _____,   *Norway*

Argentina

Colombia   **PEACE**   *United States*

                                                       Denmark
Our class has been learning about PEACE. We believe that it is
important to spread the word—it's time for PEACE!

Australia   We would like to share our studies with you. Please join us on   *Finland*

_____ at _____
         Date/Time   *Room*

Sincerely yours, _____

Georgia   Egypt   Ethiopia   Greece   England   Austria   Japan   Russia

Weather Effects

Weather is the condition of the atmosphere at a particular moment. Right now it may be bright and sunny, but quick-moving clouds could bring a thunderstorm and a sudden drop in temperature. The weather effects us and our environment in many ways. These simple experiments will help you understand how.

Icy Power

Purpose: To observe some properties of ice.

Materials: empty plastic container with lid; water; a freezer

Procedure: Fill the container to the brim with water and cover tightly with the lid. Place it in the freezer overnight. Before removing the container from the freezer predict what has happened.

Observation: After the water froze it expanded so much that it pushed the lid off the container.

Applications: 1) Fill ice cube trays only half-full; the water will expand to the top as it freezes. 2) Ice that forms in plumbing pipes may split open the pipes; prevent this by wrapping them during cold weather.

Erosion

Purpose: To observe how the running water of river erodes or "wears away" its banks.

Materials: a piece of heavy cardboard cut from a box; dampened sand or soil; pitcher or water

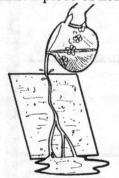

Procedure: Assemble all the materials outdoors. Coat the entire surface of the cardboard with the damp sand or soil. Form a landscape of hills and valleys. Prop up the board at one end so it remains slanted. Slowly pour water from the pitcher onto the top, middle section of the board and watch the water make a path to the bottom of the board. Watch what happens. Now tilt the board slightly to one side as you continue to pour water. **Observations:** The water constructs its own path down the slope carrying particles of the sand and soil as it goes. This is erosion in action. When the board is tilted to the side, the river finds a new course.

Application: Build a house or other structure well away from the banks of a river to avoid erosion and possibly cave-ins.

Greenhouse Effect

Purpose: To show the build-up of heat around the earth's atmosphere.

Materials: two small glass jars, both half-full or water, two thermometers; one plastic bag

Procedure: Cover one jar loosely with the plastic bag. Place both jars in the sun for at least one hour. Before taking the temperature of both jars of water, predict which one will be warmer.

Observation: The temperature of the water in the covered jar is higher.

Application: The plastic bag represents the gases formed from the fuels that are burned and released into the atmosphere. These gases have built up a layer that keeps the heat in and consequently warms the earth. If the earth is not allowed to cool down as much as it needs to, this global warming could eventually cause the polar ice caps to melt. The resulting rise in sea level could flood many cities.

Biome Chart

A biome is made up of a geographical region and the plants and animals that inhabit it. Climate largely determines which plants and animals thrive in a specific environment. Each kind of animal is suited only to a certain climate. An Arctic hare, for example, would not survive long in a tropical forest. There are six main types of biomes - Arctic tundra and ice, forest, desert, rain forest, grassland, and ocean. In general, these biomes follow the pattern of the climate zones (see diagram on page 66). Determine which biome(s) your assigned country encompasses and find out the names of ten animals that live there. Write the names on the proper section of the chart. Research the other biomes and write three animals' names in each one.

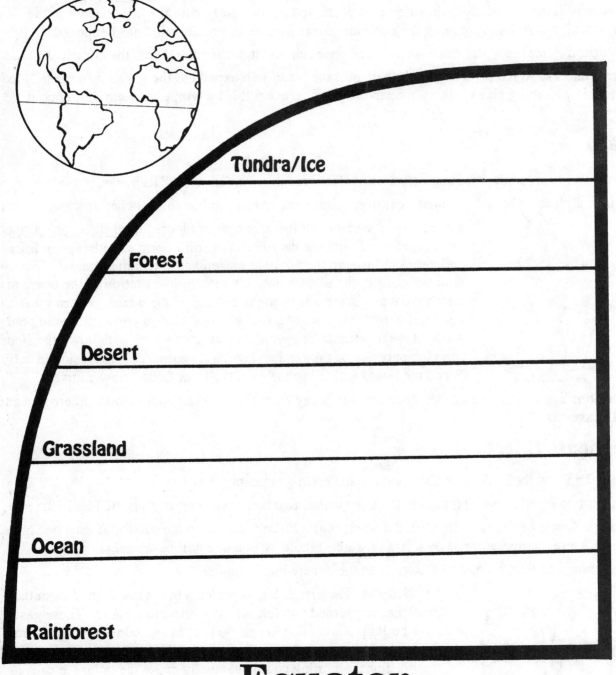

Equator

A Peace Bulletin Board

This open book bulletin board subtly suggests that students can write a new chapter in history - that of world peace. Use the bulletin board to help set the stage for a unit about peace; add to it throughout the unit. Directions, purposes, and a diagram can be found below while the open book pattern can be seen on pages 74 to 77.

Materials: Light blue butcher paper; stapler; scissors; blue construction paper; clear tape; black marking pen

Directions:

- Line the bulletin board background with the blue butcher paper; staple in place.
- Reproduce the open book pattern (pages 74 to 77) onto white copy paper.
- Cut out the book pattern and assemble as directed.
- Staple to the bulletin board background.
- Cut strips from the blue construction paper and with the marking pen write a title.
- **Note:** You may tape the strips together or write each word of the title on a separate strip (see diagram at right).
- Attach the title to the top of the book pages.

Peace Begins	With You

or

Peace	Begins
With	You

Purposes:

- Display the bulletin board prior to beginning the peace unit to spark student interest.
- Use the bulletin board to display the student's work.
- Change the title of the bulletin board to reflect other topics within the unit.
- Develop an interactive teaching tool. Write questions on index cards and place them randomly on the left page. Write answers on separate index cards; place them randomly on the right page. Call on students to read a question and find its answer. Questions and answers can be changed daily or weekly. Give student groups each a turn in composing questions and the corresponding answers. For a list of prepared questions see *What Is War? What Is Peace?* by Richard Rabinowitz (Avon Books, 1991)

Idea:

- To make a portable and reusable bulletin board assemble the book pages onto a large sheet of blue posterboard (available in art supply stores). Laminate for more durability. Write on the laminate with wipe-off pens or regular markers. To remove marker ink, use a cloth and wipe with nail polish remover, rubbing alcohol, powdered cleanser or ditto fluid. Be sure to do this in a well-ventilated area.

Diagram:

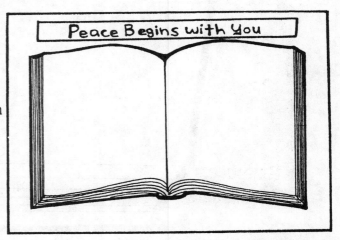

A Peace Bulletin Board *(cont.)*

Side A

Glue Tab C under Side C

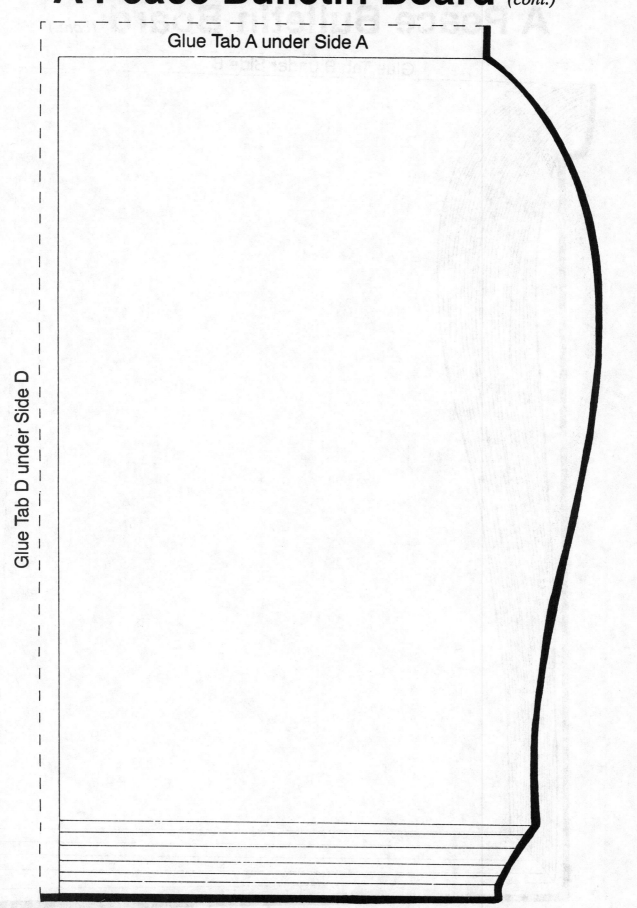

Glue Tab A under Side A

Glue Tab D under Side D

A Peace Bulletin Board *(cont.)*

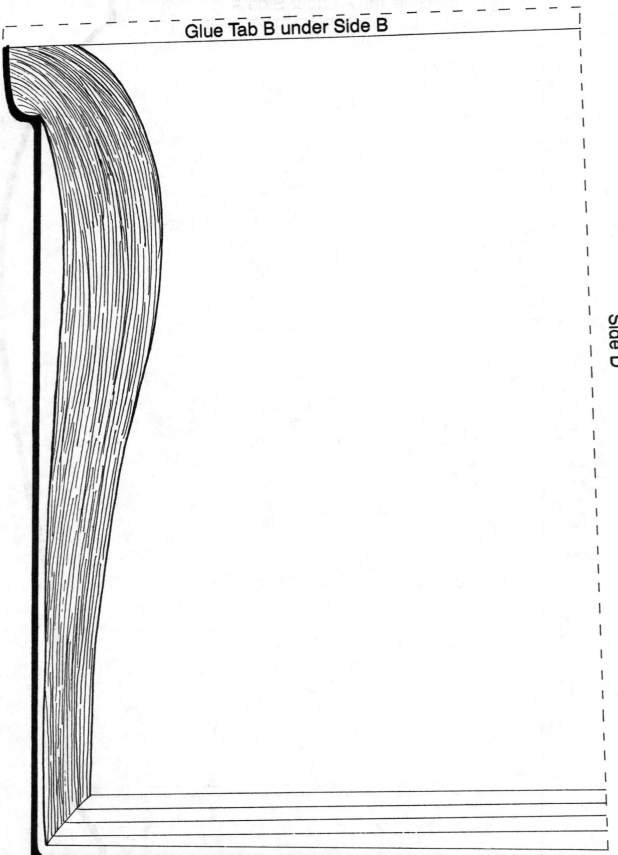

Glue Tab B under Side B

Side D

76

A Peace Bulletin Board *(cont.)*

Side B

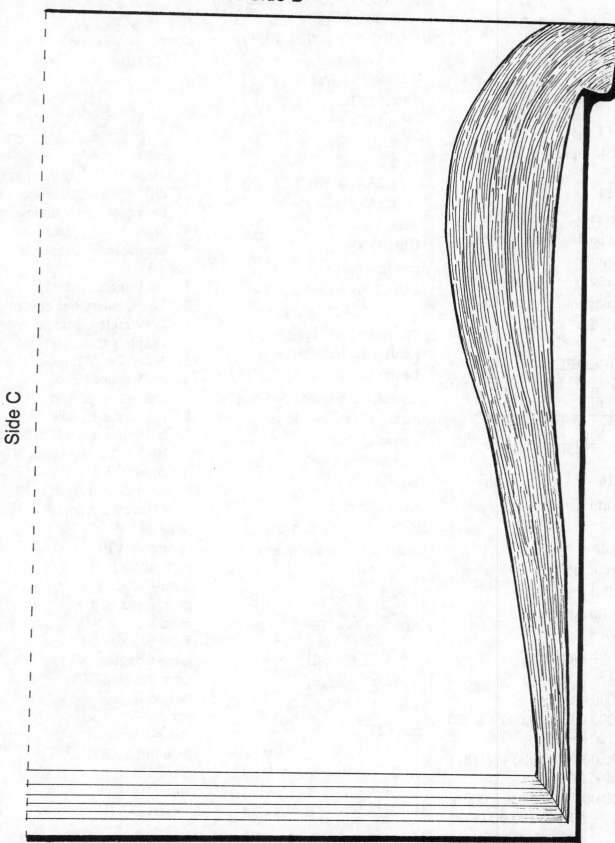

Side C

Answer Key

page 10

1. G	7. D
2. D	8. G
3. D	9. D
4. D	10. G
5. G	11. G
6. G	12. D

page 12

Peace, like charity, begins at home.

page 14

1. larder	7. willed
2. trudged	8. dumbstruck
3. dwindle	9. snare
4. wicked	10. dimwitted
5. stronghold	11. lavish
6. dainties	12. folly

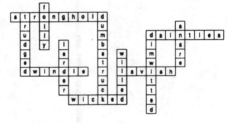

page 16

1. Northeast
2. east
3. south
4. Arctic; Pacific
5. Pribilof
6. North American
7. south
8. North America

page 19

1. 4,000+100+8
2. 1,000,000 + 70,000 + 8,000 + 100+60+2
3. 200,000 + 10,000 + 1,000 + 300+20+4
4. 300,000 + 60,000+ 3,000 + 800 + 40 + 7; 100,000 +

30,000 + 3,000+800 +20+1
5. 100,000+50,000+7,000+500 + 30 + 0
6. 300,000+20,000+700+10
   a. Vietnam
   b. World War II
   c. 52,510
   d. 1,074,054
   e. 497,668
   f. 215,632
   g. 23,470
   h. 163,180

page 21

Chrissy's

two fat pillows

a small rug with fringe

walls painted bright blue

two shiny brass hinges

small brass bell that rang

Leah's

portraits of beautiful women

curtains at the windows

a bowl of fruit

boards were crooked

Both

Keep Out sign

built with wood boards

had a ladder to her tree house

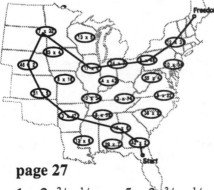

page 27

1. $2; {}^2/_4 = {}^1/_2$
2. $2; {}^2/_{16} = {}^1/_8$
3. $2; {}^2/_8 = {}^1/_4$
4. $2; {}^2/_{10} = {}^1/_5$
5. $3; {}^3/_{21} = {}^1/_7$
6. $5; {}^5/_{10} = {}^1/_2$
7. $2; {}^2/_6 = {}^1/_3$
8. ${}^4/_{12} = {}^1/_3$

page 31

page 33

1. wonderful	6. common
2. different	7. peace
3. harmony	8. amicably
4. hate	9. argue
5. separated	10. secure

page 37

1. civil rights leader
2. Montgomery bus boycott; Washington March; Poor People's Compaign
3. Nobel Peace Prize
4. civil disobedience; nonviolent protest
5. Mohandas Gandhi
6. led to passage of Civil Rights Act and voting Rights Act in 1965
7. assassinated April 4, 1968
8. I Have a Dream

page 38

excessive-VIII

prohibits-XIII

limits-XXII

guar. freedom-I

guar. women-XIX

gives accused-VI

gives Congress-XVI

guar. People-XV

people-II

persons-V

states-XIV

prohibited-XVIII

gives-XXVI

protects-IV

preserves-VII

Answer Key *(cont.)*

page 44

1. a. Japanese-Americans . .
   b. People feared and distrusted. . .
2. a. They tried to outdo...
   b. They knocked it down...
3. a. He is ordered...
   b. He is finally...
4. a. Her friend said...
   b. She became...
5. a. Islanders gave...
   b. Friends and...

page 46

Answers may vary.

page 49

1. 6   14. 10
2. 9   15. 3
3. 11   16. 15
4. 2   17. 5
5. 13   18. 12
6. 16   19. 2
7. 3   20. 1
8. 7   21. 8
9. 12   22. 6
10. 13   23. 8
11. 4   24. 14
12. 9   25. 16
13. 17

page 53

Answers may vary.

page 54

Concrete:

books; books;
volume; author; illustrators;
stories; pictures; poems;
songs; contents; celebration;
world

Abstract:

peace; themes; harmony;
understanding; beliefs; hope; all;
future

page 56

Answers may vary.

page 59

1. Jane Addams
2. Desmond Tutu
3. Andrei Sakharov
4. Lech Walesa
5. Linus Pauling

page 60

1. 6   13. 75
2. 5   14. 66
3. 14   15. 47
4. 24   16. 37
5. 33   17. 26
6. 42   18. 16
7. 52   19. 92
8. 62   20. 84
9. 72   21. 76
10. 82   22. 68
11. 83   23. 60
12. 84

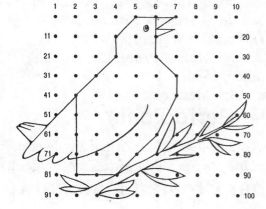

page 61

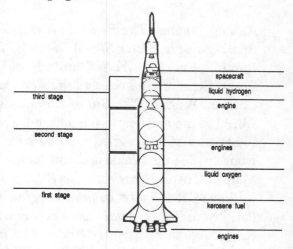

page 62

1. pacifist
2. porous
3. maladies
4. inventor
5. dynamite
6. patented
7. construction
8. destruction

Bibliography

Literature

Aaseng, Nathan. *The Peace Seekers: The Nobel Peace Prize*. Lerner Publications, 1987.

Brother Eagle, Sister Sky. A Message from Chief Seattle. Dial Books, 1991.

Bunting, Eve. *The Wall*. Clarion Books, 1990.

Coerr, Eleanor. *Sadako and the Thousand Paper Cranes*. Putnam, 1977.

Colman, Warren. *The Bill of Rights*. Children's Press, 1989.

Durrell, Ann and Marilyn Sachs, ed. *The Big Book for Peace*. Dutton Children's Books, 1990.

Fitzgerald, Merni Ingrassia. *The Peace Corps Today*. Dodd, Mead & Company, 1986.

Houston, Jeanne Wakatsuki and James D. Houston. *Farewell to Manzanar*. Houghton Mifflin, 1973.

Maruki, Toshi. *Hiroshima No Pika*. Lothrop; Lee & Shepard Books, 1980.

Millman, Dan. *Secret of the Peaceful Warrior*. H.J. Cramer, Incorporated, 1991.

Parkinson, Roger. *Attack on Pearl Harbor*. Wayland Publishers, 1973.

Ray, Deborah Kogan. *My Daddy Was a Soldier*. Holiday House, 1990.

Scholes, Katherine. *Peace Begins With You*. Sierra Club Books, 1989.

Slater, Don. *Why Do Wars Happen?* Gloucester, 1988.

Stein R. Conrad. *The Story of the United Nations*. Children's Press, 1986.

Wahl, Jan. *How the Children Stopped Wars*. Avon Books, 1969.

Biographies

Benson, Mary. *Nelson Mandela*. Hamish Hamilton, 1987.

Celsi, Teresa. *Rosa Parks and the Montgomery Bus Boycott*. Millbrook Press, 1991.

Darby, Jean. *Martin Luther King, Jr*. Lerner Publications, 1990.

Giff, Patricia Reilly. *Mother Teresa: Sister to the Poor*. Viking, 1986.

I.E. Levine. *Champion of World Peace: Dag Hammerskjöld*. Julian Messner, Incorporated 1962.

Meltzer, Milton. *Winnie Mandela: The Soul of South Africa*. Viking, 1986.

Montgomery, Elizabeth Rider. *Chief Seattle*. Garrard Publishing, 1966.

Patrick, Diane. *Martin Luther King, Jr*. Franklin Watts, 1990.

Rosen, Deborah Nodler. *Anwar El-Sadat: A Man of Peace*. Children's Press, 1986.

Spink, Kathryn. *Gandhi*. Hamish Hamilton, 1984.

Sullivan, George. *Mikhail Gorbachev*. Julian Messner, 1988.

Periodicals

News for Kids. D.M. Publishing, Incorporated 19742 MacArthur Boulevard, Irvine, CA 92715.

Planet Three: The Earth-Based Magazine for Kids. P.O. Box 52, Montgomery, VT 05470

Teacher Created Materials

TCM 112   *Great Americans*

TCM 113   *Hooray for the USA*

TCM 163   *Writing a Country Report*

TCM 280   *Friends* (A Thematic Unit)

TCM 286   *Ecology* (A Thematic Unit)

TCM 018   *Masterpiece of the Month*

TCM 314   *Literature & Critical Thinking* (contains *Sadako and the Thousand Paper Cranes*)

TCM 316   *Literature and Critical Thinking* (contains *Martin Luther King: The Peaceful Warrior*)

TCM 755   *Earth* (shape note pad)

TCM 780   *World* (jumbo shape note pad)